Best Practices *for* Teacher Leadership

*What Award-Winning
Teachers Do for Their
Professional Learning Communities*

Randi Stone Pru Cuper

CORWIN PRESS
A SAGE Publications Company
Thousand Oaks, California

Copyright © 2006 by Corwin Press.

All rights reserved. When forms and sample documents are included, their use is authorized only by educators, local school sites, and/or noncommercial or nonprofit entities who have purchased the book. Except for that usage, no part of this book may be reproduced or utilized in any form or by any means, electronic or mechanical, including photocopying, recording, or by any information storage and retrieval system, without permission in writing from the publisher.

For information:

Corwin Press
A Sage Publications Company
2455 Teller Road
Thousand Oaks, California 91320
www.corwinpress.com

Sage Publications Ltd.
1 Oliver's Yard
55 City Road
London EC1Y 1SP
United Kingdom

Sage Publications India Pvt. Ltd.
B-42, Panchsheel Enclave
Post Box 4109
New Delhi 110 017 India

Printed in the United States of America

Library of Congress Cataloging-in-Publication Data

Stone, Randi.
Best practices for teacher leadership: What award-winning teachers do for their professional learning communities / Randi Stone, Prudence H. Cuper.
      p. cm.
Includes index.
ISBN 1-4129-1579-1 (cloth : alk. paper)—ISBN 1-4129-1580-5 (pbk. : alk. paper)
    1. Teacher effectiveness—United States. 2. Effective teaching—United States.
3. Educational leadership—United States. I. Cuper, Prudence H. II. Title.
LB1025.3.S755 2006
371.102—dc22

                                        2005025996

This book is printed on acid-free paper.

06   07   08   09   10   10 9 8 7 6 5 4 3 2 1

Acquisitions Editor:	Faye Zucker
Editorial Assistant:	Gem Rabanera
Production Editor:	Melanie Birdsall
Typesetter:	C&M Digitals (P) Ltd.
Copyeditor:	Diana Breti
Proofreader:	Annette Pagliaro
Indexer:	Michael Ferreira
Cover Designer:	Michael Dubowe

6140109912

371.2011

MO 5005905
6/7/06
£23.

✓

Best
Practices *for*
Teacher
Leadership

University of Cumbria

Tower Hamlets Schools Library Service
Tower Hamlets Professional Development Centre
English Street, London. E3 4TA
Tel: 0207 364 6426

Other Corwin Press Books by Randi Stone

Best Classroom Management Practices for Reaching All Learners: What Award-Winning Classroom Teachers Do, 2005.

Best Teaching Practices for Reaching All Learners: What Award-Winning Classroom Teachers Do, 2004.

What?! Another New Mandate? What Award-Winning Teachers Do When School Rules Change, 2002.

Best Practices for High School Classrooms: What Award-Winning Secondary Teachers Do, 2001.

Best Classroom Practices: What Award-Winning Elementary Teachers Do, 1999.

New Ways to Teach Using Cable Television: A Step-by-Step Guide, 1997.

This book is dedicated to dearest Karen who always made everyone smile.

—Randi Stone

To my mother, Dr. Frances Hobbie (a.k.a. Gaga), the finest teacher/leader in my life.

—Pru Cuper

Contents

Preface

The finest educational leadership does not necessarily happen behind the closed doors of principals' offices or during late-night board of education meetings. In fact, some of the most dynamic leadership in schools today happens in broad daylight and with classroom doors flung wide open. It is the leadership of teachers—big-spirited, compassionate, and inventive teachers who lead through their willingness to reach out to their colleagues and their communities. It is the leadership of teachers who are always on the lookout for ways to enhance their practice through the use of new technologies, through professional development, and through discovering and sharing the talents of the people living in their communities.

In the following pages, we offer stories from across the country written by teachers who have been recognized for the unique ways in which they serve as leaders within their schools. From offering "chemmystery" experiments to finding their "lost Dutchmen" to bringing "Sweet Home Chicago" to Room 13, the stories that follow are inspiring and unique. We hope you enjoy them.

Acknowledgments

Thank you to an outstanding group of teachers for sharing your stories with us. You stand at the educational "front line" and offer inspiration to so many people: other teachers, parents, community members, and, most of all, the children in your classrooms.

About the Authors

Randi Stone is a graduate of Clark University, Boston University, and Salem State College. She completed her doctorate in education at the University of Massachusetts, Lowell. She is the author of seven books with Corwin Press including her latest publication, *Best Classroom Management Practices for Reaching All Learners*. She lives with her daughter, Blair, in Keene, New Hampshire.

Pru Cuper, a native of New Jersey, is an assistant professor in the Keene State College Education Department where she teaches elementary methods and child development classes. Before earning her PhD at North Carolina State University, Pru and her husband raised their three children (Prue Jr., Marcus, and Will) while Pru worked as a middle school reading and language arts teacher. Pru's current work, published in academic journals and presented at national conferences, focuses on literacy and teacher education reform.

About the Contributors

Nancy K. Ackerman, Reading Process Trainer
Santa Teresa Elementary
201 Comerciantes
Santa Teresa, NM 88008
Phone: (505) 589-3445
E-mail: nackerman@gisd.k12.nm.us

Number of Years Teaching: 28
Awards: New Mexico State Teacher of the Year (2004)
Gadsden Independent School District Teacher
of the Year (2003)
Ysleta Independent School District Top 5 Elementary
Teachers of the Year (1993)

Roxie R. Albrecht, Second-Grade Teacher
Robert Frost Elementary
3101 S. 4th Ave.
Sioux Falls, SD 57105
School Phone: (605) 367-6170
E-mail: ahlbrecr@sf.k12.sd.us

Number of Years Teaching: 30
Awards: South Dakota Teacher of the Year (2004)
Presidential Award for Excellence in Mathematics and
Science Teaching (2002)
National Board Certified Teacher–Middle Childhood Generalist
(2001)

Lisa Alvey, Fourth-Grade Teacher
Heath Elementary Schools
4365 Metropolis Lake Rd.
West Paducah, KY 42086
School Phone: (270) 538-4060
E-mail: lalvey@mccracken.k12.ky.us

Number of Years Teaching: 20

Linda Antinone, Mathematics and Physics Teacher
R.L. Paschal High School
3001 Forest Park Blvd.
Fort Worth, TX 76110
School Phone: (817) 922-6600
E-mail: lanti@ftworth.isd.tenet.edu

Number of Years Teaching: 19
Awards: Radio Shack National Teacher Award (2004)
Fort Worth ISD Secondary Teacher of the Year (1995)
Presidential Award for Excellence in Mathematics
Teaching (1993)

Deidre Austen, Fourth-Grade Teacher
Lutherville Laboratory School for Science, Mathematics,
and Communication
1700 York Rd.
Lutherville, MD 21093
School Phone: (410) 887-7800
E-mail: dausten@bcps.org

Number of Years Teaching: 15
Award: Milken National Educator Award (2004)

Janet Barnstable, Communications Resource Teacher, Grades 7 and 8
Percy Julian Middle School
416 S. Ridgeland
Oak Park, IL 60302
School Phone: (708) 524-3040
E-mail: jbarnstable@op97.org

Number of Years Teaching: 43

Awards: Global SchoolNet Online Shared Learning Award Finalist
(2002–2004)

Larry Stilgebauer Award—Excellence in Technology
Integration (2000)

Golden Apple Award Finalist/Excellence
in Teaching (1996)

Mary Catherine Bradshaw, AP U.S. History; Language and
Composition; American Studies; and International
Baccalaureate, History of the Americas, English,
IB Coordinator
    Hillsboro Comprehensive High School
    3812 Hillsboro Rd.
    Nashville, TN 37215
    School Phone: (615) 298-8400
    E-mail: marycatbrad@yahoo.com

Awards: Gilder Lehrman Preserve American History Award,
Tennessee (2004)

National Council for the Social Studies High School
Outstanding Teacher (1995)

Disney American Teacher Award (1994)

Charla Bunker, Fifth-Grade Teacher
    West Elementary School
    1205 1st Ave. NW
    Great Falls, MT 59404
    School Phone: (406) 268-7204
    E-mail: char_bunker@gfps.k12.mt.us

Number of Years Teaching: 22

Awards: Toyota Tapestry Grant (2004)

ING Unsung Heroes Award (2003)

State Presidential Award for Excellence in Science and
Mathematics Teaching (2002)

Alisia Carey, Preschool Special Education Teacher
Oak Grove Elementary
479 Oak Drive
Lexington, SC 29073
School Phone: (803) 356-0220
E-mail: acarey@lexington1.net

Number of Years Teaching: 20
Awards: Shaklee Institute Exceptional Teaching Award (2004)
             National Board Certification—Exceptional Needs (2000)

Michael Corcoran, District Science Research Coordinator
Dickinson High School
2 Palisade Ave.
Jersey City, NJ 07002
School Phone: (201) 714-4402
E-mail: PARISBAY@aol.com

Number of Years Teaching: 25+
Awards: All USA National Teacher Team (2003)
             Princeton U. Prize for Distinguished Secondary School
                 Teaching in NJ (2003)
             Hudson County (NJ) Teacher of the Year (1994, 2001)

Maria Jose De la Torre, Fourth-Grade Teacher
Collinswood Dual Language Academy
12150 St. Emilion Place
Pineville, NC 28134
School Phone: (980) 343-5820
E-mail: Maria.delatorre@cms.k12.nc.us

Number of Years Teaching: 12
Awards: Crystal Apple National Teacher Award
                 (2002, 2003, 2004)
             Creative Ideas from Our Teachers Contest,
                 Idea Book For Educators (2002, 2004)
             Honourable Mention, National Kind
                 Teacher Award (2004)

Erica Drennan, First-Grade Teacher
Confidence Elementary
HC 63 Box
163 Red House
Red House, WV 25168
School Phone: (304) 586-2041
E-mail: ericadrennan@yahoo.com

Number of Years Teaching: 4
Award: ING Unsung Heroes (2004)

Michelle Evans, Sixth-Grade Teacher
Valley Elementary School
7436 East 200 South
Huntsville, UT 84317
School Phone: (801) 452-4180
E-mail: smevans@wsdmail.net

Number of Years Teaching: 18
Awards: USA Today Teacher Team (2003)
National Milken Educator (1998)
National Presidential Award for Excellence in Math and
Science Teaching (1996)

Deborah Forringer, Teacher of Instrumental
Music, Grades 4–6
Shannock Valley Elementary School
Main St.
Rural Valley, PA 16249
School Phone: (724) 783-6991
E-mail: ford@asd.k12.pa.us

Number of Years Teaching: 30
Awards: ING Unsung Heroes (2004, 2005)
Selected to attend the Teach Vietnam Teachers Conference
in Washington, D.C. (2003)
National/State Teacher of the Year Finalist—Forringer
(1999–2000)

Jessica Galla, First-Grade Teacher
Cumberland Hill Annex
Mendon Rd.
Cumberland, RI 02864
School Phone: (401) 658-1660
E-mail: JLG919@aol.com

Number of Years Teaching: 5
Award: ING Unsung Heroes (2004)

Dennis Griner, Teacher of Current World Issues, Grade 12; U.S.
   History, Grade 11; and Audio-Visual Communications, Grades 9–12
   Garfield-Palouse High School
   600 East Alder
   Palouse, WA 99161
   School Phone: (509) 878-1921
   E-mail: dgriner@garpal.wednet.edu

Number of Years Teaching: 33
Awards: D.A.R. Washington State History Teacher of the Year (2004)
           Finalist, National Teacher of the Year (2004)
           Washington State Teacher of the Year (2004)

Tammy Haggerty Jones, Third-Grade Teacher
Strassburg Elementary
2002 E. 223 St.
Sauk Village, IL
School Phone: (708) 758-4754
E-mail: Upontheroof24@aol.com

Number of Years Teaching: 4
Awards: Fulbright Memorial Program for Teachers (2005)
           Disney American Teacher Award (2004)

Jason R. Harding, Learning Support Services, Grades K–5
North Allegheny School
216 Rush Valley Rd.
Monroeville, PA 15146
School Phone: (412) 372-0184
E-mail: jharding@northallegheny.org

Number of Years Teaching: 4
Awards: Disney Teacher Award (2004)
          North Allegheny Distinguished Leadership Award (2004)
          Marie McKay Education Award (2000)

Keil Hileman, Social Studies, Museum Studies, Grades 6–8
    Monticello Trails Middle School
    6100 Monticello Rd.
    Shawnee, KS 66226
    School Phone: (913) 422-1100
    E-mail: keilh@usd232.org

Number of Years Teaching: 13
Award: Kansas State Teacher of the Year (2004)

Linda Hodges, Science Department Chair, Grades 9–12;
  Honors Biology; AP Biology
    Rosary High School
    1340 N. Acacia Ave.
    Fullerton, CA 92831
    School Phone: (714) 879-6302
    E-mail: lhodges@rosaryhs.org

Number of Years Teaching: 35
Awards: Radio Shack National Teacher Award (2004)
          Who's Who Among America's Teachers (2003)
          American Red Cross Most Inspiring Teacher Award (2002)

Scott Hogan, Mathematics Teacher, Grades 9–12
    Ocotillo High School
    2616 East Greenway Rd.
    Phoenix, AZ 85032
    School Phone: (602) 765-8470
    E-mail: scott.hogan@leonagroup.com

Number of Years Teaching: An irrational number
Awards: Wells Fargo Teacher's Partner Grant (2002 and 2004)
          Arizona Heritage Project Grant (2003–2004)
          Semifinalist in NASDAQ National Teaching Awards
            Competition (2001)

Rita Cannon Hovermale, Teacher, Grades 9–12
Woodbridge High School
307 Laws St.
Bridgeville, DE 19933
School Phone: (302) 337-8289
E-mail: rhovermale@wsd.k12.de.us

Number of Years Teaching: 20
Awards: Delaware Teacher of the Year (2004)
National Board Certified Teacher (2000)

Susan Illgen, Kindergarten Teacher
Grove Lower Elementary
801 W. 10th St.
Grove, OK 74345
School Phone: (918) 786-5573
E-mail: j.s.illgen@sbcglobal.net

Number of Years Teaching: 6
Awards: Oklahoma State Teacher of the Year (2005)
Smarter Kids Foundation Excellence in Teaching
Award (2005)
Six Time Grant Recipient, Grove Educational Foundation
for Excellence (2001–2004)

Angela Judd, English Teacher, Grades 11–12
Hutchinson High School
1200 Roberts Rd.
Hutchinson, MN 55350
School Phone: (320) 587-2151
E-mail: angiej@hutch.k12.mn.us

Number of Years Teaching: 30
Awards: Minnesota Teacher of the Year Semifinalist (2005)
Minnesota Academic Excellence Foundation Teacher
Achievement Award (2004)
Hutchinson Schools Teacher of the Year (2004)

Jonathan Kern, School Standards Coach
Landon Middle School
1819 Thacker Ave.
Jacksonville, FL 32207
School Phone: (904) 346-5650
E-mail: kernj@educationcentral.org

Number of Years Teaching: 7
Awards: Milken Family Foundation Award (2004)
Region V, Duval County Public Schools Teacher
of the Year (2003)
Region I, Duval County Public Schools Teacher
of the Year (2001)

Linda Keteyian, Science Teacher, Grades 3–5
Higgins Elementary
9200 Olivet
Detroit, MI 49209
School Phone: (313) 849-1167
E-mail: keteyian@yahoo.com

Number of Years Teaching: 20
Awards: ING Unsung Heroes (2004)
Earthwatch Fellow (2001, 2003, 2004)
Eleanor Roosevelt Fellowship (2002)

Kristy Kidd, Sixth-Grade Teacher
Dunbar Magnet Middle School
1100 Wright Ave.
Little Rock, AR 72206
School Phone: (501) 447-2643
E-mail: kiddzoo@aol.com

Number of Years Teaching: 13
Awards: Milken National Educator Award (2004)
Dunbar Magnet Middle School Teacher
of the Year (2003)

Trudy Lund, Kindergarten Teacher
   Airport Heights Elementary
   Anchorage, AK 99508
   School Phone: (907) 742-4550
   E-mail: lund_tracy@asdk12.org

Number of Years Teaching: 20
Award: State of Alaska Teacher of the Year from the
             Wal-Mart/Sam's Club Foundation (2002)

Hillary Mason, Fifth-Grade Teacher
   Oxbow Community School
   100 Oxbow Lake Rd.
   White Lake, MI 48386
   School Phone: (248) 684-8084
   E-mail: masonh@huronvalley.k12.mi.us

Number of Years Teaching: 2

Chris McAuliffe, Fifth-Grade Teacher
   Oxbow Community School
   White Lake, MI 48386
   School Phone: (248) 684-8084
   E-mail: mcauliffec@huronvalley.k12.mi.us

Number of Years Teaching: 17
Awards: Milken National Educator Award (2004)
             Michigan Teacher of the Year finalist (2003)
             Oakland County Teacher of the Year finalist (2002)
             WDIV Outstanding Teacher Award (2001)

Evan D. Mortenson, Sixth-Grade Teacher
   Conger Elementary
   1700 California Ave.
   Klamath Falls, OR 97601
   School Phone: (541) 883-4772
   E-mail: evanmortenson@kfall.k12.or.us

Number of Years Teaching: 14
Award: Phi Delta Kappa/Wal-Mart Oregon State
             Teacher of the Year (2002)

Karen Neely, Science Teacher, Grades 10–12
Pearl High School
500 Pirate Cove Rd.
Pearl, MS 39208
School Phone: (601) 932-7931
E-mail: kneely@pearl.k12.ms.us

Awards: Mississippi Alternate Teacher of the Year (2004–2005)
Third Congressional Teacher of the Year (2004–2005)
Metro Teacher of the Year (1998)

Diane Marie Palmer-Furman, Third-Grade Teacher
Schenck Elementary
1300 Lowell Blvd.
Denver, CO 80219
School Phone: (303) 935-6506
E-mail: diane_palmer@dpsk12.org

Number of Years Teaching: 12
Awards: Milken Family Foundation National Educator Award (2004)
Who's Who Among America's Teachers (2000, 2004)

Laura Partridge, Eighth-Grade Mathematics
Swanson Middle School
5800 N. Washington Blvd.
Arlington, VA 22205
School Phone: (703) 228-5500
E-mail: Laura_Partridge@apsva.us.edu

Number of Years Teaching: 6
Awards: The Washington Post Agnes Meyer Outstanding
Teacher Award (2004)
Arlington County Teacher of the Year (2004)

Michal Robinson, Science Chair; Biology Teacher
Huffman High School
950 Old Springville Rd.
Birmingham, AL 35215
School Phone: (205) 231-5082
E-mail: mgrobinson@bhamcityschools.org

Number of Years Teaching: 26

Awards: AAUW Eleanor Roosevelt Project Implementation
            Grant (2003, 2004)
            Radio Shack National Teacher Award (2004)
            Birmingham City Schools Teacher of the Year (2003)

Frank Rossi, Chairperson, Business and Technology
  Education, Grades 11–12
    Notre Dame High School
    24 Ricardo St.
    West Haven, CT 06516
    School Phone: (203) 933-1673
    E-mail: frossi@notredamchs.com

Number of Years Teaching: 6

Award: National Council on Economic Education NASDAQ
            National Teaching Award Northeast Regional
            Semifinalist (2002, 2003, 2004)

Ernest Schiller, Biology Teacher, Grades 9–12
    Central Lee High School
    2642 Highway 218
    Donnellson, IA 52625
    School Phone: (319) 835-5121
    E-mail: crnestschiller@hotmail.com

Number of Years Teaching: 34

Awards: Iowa Teacher of the Year (2004)
            Iowa Academy of Science Distinguished Service
            Award (2001)
            Presidential Award for Excellence in Science
            Teaching (1995)

Eileen Serene, Learning Support, Grades 4–6
    Shannock Valley Elementary School
    Main St.
    Rural Valley, PA 16249
    School Phone: (724) 783-6991
    E-mail: sere@asd.k12.pa.us

Number of Years Teaching: 17

Awards: ING Unsung Heroes (2004, 2005)
              Selected to attend the Teach Vietnam Teachers Conference
                 in Washington, D.C. (2002)
              Armstrong School District Teacher of the
                 Year—Serene (2000)

Christopher R. Shadle, Third-Grade Teacher
   Bowers Elementary School
   1041 32nd St. NW
   Massillon, OH 44647
   Phone: (330) 830-1847
   E-mail: CtnOH44709@aol.com

Number of Years Teaching: 24

Awards and Grants: Martha Holden Jennings Grant (1999–2002)
                        Ohio Arts Council Integration Project
                           (2003, 2004)
                        NEA Innovation Grant (2004)

Stacey Smiar, Science Teacher, Grades 5–8
   Fayerweather St. School
   765 Concord Ave.
   Cambridge, MA 02138
   School Phone: (617) 876-4745
   E-mail: ssmiar@hotmail.com

Number of Years Teaching: 10

Awards: Toyota Tapestry Grant Winner (2004)
              Earthwatch Educator's Fellowship (2004)
              Fulbright Memorial Fund
                 Teacher Program (2003)

Diane Woodford, Fifth-Grade Teacher
   Covington Elementary School
   2116 A Street
   South Sioux City, NE 68776
   School Phone: (402) 494-4238
   E-mail: diane.woodford@ssccardinals.org

Number of Years Teaching: 30

Awards: Who's Who Among America's Educators (2005)
Nebraska Teacher of Excellence (2004)
Nebraska Teacher of the Year (2004)

Julie York, Teacher of Video Productions, Grades 9–12
South Portland High School
Portland, ME 04106
School Phone: (207) 767-3266
E-mail: yorkju@spsd.org

Number of Years Teaching: 4

Awards: Cable in the Classroom National Leaders in
Learning (2005)
Radio Shack National Teacher Award (2004)
Time Warner Crystal Apple Award (2004)

CHAPTER 1

Leading Through Collaboration With Colleagues

⬚ Excellence in Education

Trudy Lund
Anchorage, Alaska

A common joke among teachers is that people think we come to school each day to play with the children. Yes, I've been known to play with my students. (In fact, today I pretended to eat a Play-Doh "cookie" in order to please a sweet kindergartner.) Those who have taught for any length of time know that teaching is a very stressful occupation. Add to that the pressure of ongoing standardized testing requirements and many wonderful teachers, unfortunately, leave the profession. I hope you will glean something helpful from what I have learned about teaching and life during the past 20+ years.

Be an Excellent Teacher

Teaching could be a 24/7 job if you wanted it to be. I suppose you could do that if you didn't want a life or a family. However, remember that if you are married, your family does come first. As I journeyed through 20 years of teaching, I saw many who were on every committee, taught every training day, and had their name on most district publications. Almost 100% of those teachers' marriages have ended in divorce. Your classroom will take most of your time. Yes, teach a class from time to time. Take classes to keep you inspired with fresh ideas. If you have to introduce yourself to your husband and children, you're doing too much.

File folders and file boxes are your best friends. Don't keep reinventing the wheel each year. That's not to say you want to do the same things year in and year out, you don't. But there will be some really cool projects that you'll want to do each year, and if you're organized, you can pull them out and be ready to go. I have a file box and an artist's folder for each month of the year. I would probably go back into my burning house to save them (I'm kidding). But keeping my things organized has saved me hundreds of hours each year.

One day after school I wandered into the room of a co-worker and dear friend. As she talked to me, I watched her go around the perimeter of the room, organizing and putting away the clutter of the day. I was amazed and said, "Do you do this every night?" She said, "Yes. Another teacher told me to never leave until I'd cleaned around the room and cleared my desk." What wonderful advice! I follow it every afternoon and I look forward to coming in the next day.

Share Your Excellence With Others

The best classes and seminars I've ever taken were taught by other teachers. I've taught some myself. I chuckle when I think about that 21-year-old young woman who graduated after 3½ years of college.

What I knew then compared to what I know now are miles apart. Most of what I've learned about teaching I've learned from other teachers. Don't be afraid to ask your co-workers for help. During my first years of teaching, I carried a camera around with me (an idea from another teacher.) I took pictures of classroom set-ups, art projects, and bulletin boards. I still have those pictures and have used many of those ideas. If math is your favorite subject to teach and you've mastered a particularly difficult curriculum, volunteer to share your ideas with other teachers.

About 15 years ago, we adopted a new reading curriculum. The "whole language" concept was so new to everyone that we felt we were drowning. We formed a first-grade teacher support group. Initially, we met to discuss how to teach the new curriculum. After a few meetings, it turned into a sharing of ideas about the entire first-grade curriculum. We started bringing in ideas each month and providing a copy for each member of the group. After meeting all year, we went away with a bundle of ideas, and we felt comfortable with the new reading curriculum. If you're feeling uneasy in an area of the curriculum, chances are so are many other teachers. Invite other grade-level teachers in your area to meet once a month. Serve bagels and share your fears and cheers. Your colleagues are your greatest resource.

Be an Excellent Co-worker

I want my classroom to be a stress reliever for my co-workers and myself. I'm not sure why, but for the first 10 or so years of teaching, I viewed my classroom as a bedroom at a friend's house. I felt I was a guest and should keep everything tidy and my personal belongings in a suitcase. It probably sounds silly, but I remember the day I excitedly put an adhesive-backed mirror inside my teacher's closet. I began to realize that I spent more waking hours in that room than at home, so why not make it comfortable? Hence, I began to stock my room with stress busters: a microwave, refrigerator, Ziplocs, fancy paper, a toothbrush, postage stamps, snacks, an extra set of clothes, the list goes on and on. At least once a year every teacher in my building will come in to borrow something, and I like that. I understand the pressure we work under, and it makes me feel good to make someone else's day a little easier. So, if you're still working under "guest" guidelines, stock your room with whatever makes you happy. And don't forget to share with your co-workers. Some day you'll need to borrow something from them.

Be an Excellent Friend to Families

Each September, 20 or so fresh little faces timidly walk through my classroom door. They are not only walking through that door, they (and their families) are also walking into my heart. I teach in a neighborhood where many families are struggling just to get by. I want my students and their families to view me as their friend and someone they can turn to for help. I am thankful that my husband has a generous heart. In the 28 years we've been married, he has never complained about the money I've spent on my students and their families. I know I can't cure the pain that many of these people endure, but I can help in small ways. I remember a family whose oldest child was in my class. Their younger child was born with many physical and mental challenges. I knew money was extremely tight for them. A friend of mine asked me if I knew of anyone who wanted some children's clothing, much of which was like new. I collected those clothes and took them to school. There wasn't a dry eye in the room when I asked the student if she'd like the clothes. You see, it didn't cost me anything. And on the last day of school, I received one of my most cherished letters thanking me for caring about their family.

Save Some Excellence for Yourself

A few years ago I took a class. I can't even remember what the class was about, but the instructor was talking about personality types. She had us take a test and then we scored them and identified our own personality type. She told us that approximately 7% of the U.S. population was the personality type that felt a deep responsibility to help others. It is estimated that 70% of the teachers in the United States are in this category. We care about the children and we want to help. But we must take care of ourselves, too. Let your down time be down time. Carve out time to go for walks, sit and look at a beautiful sunset, and yes, stop and smell the roses.

For probably the first 10 years of my teaching career, I used to carry a heavy burden about all the children in the world. I worried about those who weren't getting an adequate education. I felt it was my responsibility to make sure that happened. I felt I had to do something. One day I read a story about a little boy standing on a beach, throwing in sea stars that had washed up on the shore. A man walked by and said, "Why are you throwing back sea stars? There are so many! You can't possibly make a difference." The boy looked at the man, held up the sea star in his hand, and as he tossed it back into the water he said, "I made a difference to this one!"

Each year we get a classroom of sea stars. I can't be responsible for all the children on earth, just those in my room. Make sure all your sea stars end up in the ocean. You will make a difference to each one of them!

Lovingly dedicated to Jerry H. I will *never* forget you, buddy!

Operation ~~Help Me!~~ Collaboration

Or How I Survived My First Years of Teaching

Julie York
Portland, Maine

Let me start by saying I am not a trained professional; I am in training. I didn't go to school to teach high school, nor did I prepare myself to deal with the complications that arise from such a profession. I got in through a stroke of luck and ability and have never looked back. How did I survive? How did I adapt? Because I'm Wonder Woman! Well, actually, I'd like to think it's because of a little thing called "collaboration." I collaborated with a *lot* of people.

Before I even began my illustrious career as a video productions teacher, real life instructor, Web master, assistant yearbook advisor, anime club creator/administrator, and educational access channel director (whoa, when did those titles pile on?) there was Scott. Scott met me the week after the principal called to inform me that I had the job. This was a job I didn't expect to get based on skill alone, especially since I was trained for elementary school and had little to no experience with "the big kids." Sure, I knew the equipment and the subject, but the job? That's where Scott came in. He showed me the ropes, explained the position, and helped me better understand the curriculum he left behind when he left to teach Woodworking. We collaborated, or at least, I tried. Mostly I just sat and listened as if I were a rather large sponge. I was there, he was there, and he had experience. It comforted me to know that if I needed help there was someone, somewhere I could go to. Okay, so it wasn't collaboration per se, but it was definitely me working together with someone else. I would have helped more if I had half the experience under my belt that Scott had.

But I definitely couldn't stay that way forever. After struggling through the fateful first year of teaching, I began to grow and develop as a professional. The kids became used to me, I became used to them, and I began to care less about just getting through the lessons and more about the quality of the course. (Trust me, first year teachers of the world, it happens!) Students started to share ideas with me and I started to notice that their ideas made sense and could be used to better my plans. I began to think about ways to develop the curriculum and strategies to involve even more people, other people, specifically those persons *outside* my classroom. I was getting tired of having everything be from me and my experiences, and the course work remaining the same old routine. This is where my department chair, Jerry, stepped in.

Jerry and I shared a video course the second semester of my first year. It was amazing! Suddenly I could bounce around ideas with another teacher who was actually teaching the same course that I was. We shared curriculum, discussed ideas, and worked together. Our students collaborated and worked in groups across classes. Work and lessons became more vivid and detailed, and curriculum was enhanced. The lesson plans were dusted off and rubrics were updated once a semester. Students started to notice that the videos we created had more variety and a greater impact.

Life was good!

I began to work with other teachers to see how they taught things. During lunch break, I would chat with Ralph from science in an effort to better understand how he dealt with the physics of light and color temperature. During department prep, I would talk with the retiree Jack about how he worked with particularly pesky kids, the ones who know all the right buttons to press and exactly when to press them. Life was getting less hectic, and I thought, "Hey, I'll be ready for year two! I have help, I'm getting better at this, and I can do it!"

That's when a brand new class was added to my load: Computer Applications 1. Once more I was put in the position of knowing the content but not knowing how to teach it. This time there happened to be a few teachers who taught the class but no concrete curriculum. In addition, the state started to discuss the Maine Learning Results and Common Assessments. As a school and as a state we needed to work together to present a curriculum all students could achieve. We were responsible for really nailing down our rubrics and producing something we could show the big people in Augusta.

This was when collaboration came in once more to save the day. This was when I started working with Sheree. Together we plowed through it all and made something to be proud of. We developed a system of rubrics that worked well across all our classes, created a curriculum for Computer Applications 1 that was based on what we'd had in place but with some details ironed out, and even had time for the occasional chat or sharing of experiences. I helped her and she helped me. Besides Jerry from last semester, this was my first real experience at having a say in something beyond what came out of my mouth in my courses. I was collaborating! Because of my work with Sheree, I learned how to create a more solid curriculum, improving the one I already had for the video course. I overcame the stress of having nothing and worked with someone else to create something we could both be proud of.

Working together was interesting, too. I learned that sometimes I would do more work and other times she'd do more. It didn't always end up equal, especially when we had Jerry working with us for another course. Dividing a task by three is a lot more complicated than dividing by two, and no one who deals with teenagers all day long can be patient all the time. Collaboration means learning to work with others just as much as it means working for a better quality. I learned as much about myself as I did about learning to work with people. It's easier for me now because I understand the politics of working in a group of adult professionals. If you've never done it, do it. Trust me, it can be hard, stressful, and at the same time, rewarding. Just like the groups of students we sometimes force to work together, adults can learn to do it when there's a goal in sight.

So by the time the second half of my second year rolled around, I was ready and pumped to do more work with other teachers. I started doing projects with the rest of the school. My students started airing more and more work on the educational access channel. I started inviting community members into the classroom to discuss various issues and concepts. I started to really listen to those around me and learn. I started to talk back. I started to work with others, enjoying it and allowing it to enhance my work. I also wasn't frantically trying to make it through my first year, half sick the whole time and desperately trying to get better while losing more and more sleep.

Who knows what did it, but I started to become part of the team of South Portland High School. I was becoming part of a community of teachers dedicated to teaching young people and helping them develop. There was no single leader but, rather, a community of teachers that together led the students, each other, and the school.

I don't think I'll ever look at teaching the same way again. Now I don't just teach one class, I work in a class that is connected to a building that is filled with possibilities. I don't just check with my department chair when considering a new project; I check with other teachers and sometimes even the principal. I don't do it every single lesson (where would I find the time?), but I do try to find the time. I try to find the opportunities for collaboration wherever and whenever I can. Voting 2004 involved my class, computer classes, English classes, social studies classes, and more. The Healthy Living Project of 2003 started as a principal-led initiative and turned into something the whole school could be proud of, including my five video classes. We interacted with each other, other students, and the community to produce some of the best public service announcements, video commercials, and instructional videos I've ever seen. We worked together—not just me and my students, but me, my students, and my school.

Collaboration brings people together. I have felt validated, secure, and happy during the times I have worked with others to create something bigger than my classroom. I have felt some of the burden and responsibilities of being a teacher lighten just from sharing them with others. Collaboration is something that now, three years later and going strong, I wouldn't do without in education.

So the next time I have to redo a curriculum from scratch because of a state mandate saying we need yet one more standard to add to the heap, I know exactly what to do. Give it a go, test it out myself, then bring it around to others. Get feedback and input and make the changes. It is my responsibility to teach my curriculum, but that doesn't mean I need to do it all alone. Once more, I am not a trained professional; I am in training.

Helpful Tips

- After you make a lesson plan or unit, show it to other people. You'll make it the best you possibly can (because who'd want to show other people something that really stinks?) and then they'll help you improve it even more. You'll be amazed at what they see.
- Listen to others. Sometimes I can't shut up and I think I know all the answers, but then I'm reminded, usually by students, that I'm not perfect. There's a time to talk and there's a time to listen. Try listening some more.
- Working together *can* be more work (like the group of kids in which one student does everything for the group), but it can also mean sharing the work and sharing the outcome. It's worth it. Don't be discouraged by bad experiences; there's always a way to make it work. Think of your students, the outcome, and getting the task completed.
- Not everything has to be done with others. Don't fix the unbroken wheel, but do look at your curriculum every now and then and think, "Is this the best it could be? Is this working well, or could it be better? If it needs improvement, do I know how or would someone else be able to see it?" It's hard to see problems when it's your creation.

Professional Collaboration Within an Inclusive Classroom Setting

How to Make It Work

Alisia Carey
Lexington, South Carolina

The concept of team teaching is inviting to some educators and daunting to others. Just the thought of sharing or relinquishing some teaching responsibilities is almost too much for some teachers to bear, and therefore they may miss out on a wonderful professional experience, one that all involved can learn from and embrace. While team teaching can be a highly motivating and fulfilling experience, it is not always easy. It takes planning, compromise, and dedication from all parties. But at its best, team teaching is an inspiring and rewarding practice for educators and students alike. This article will describe a successful team teaching situation, the collaboration it takes for it to run smoothly, and the value of this approach to all of the students involved.

As the special education teacher in an inclusive preschool child development class, I have first-hand knowledge of the challenges involved in making team teaching work. As a result of the need to provide a more appropriate setting for some students with disabilities, the inclusive preschool class was started six years ago. Because this class is the only one of its kind in our district, my co-worker and I did not have a model; we had to work together to implement the program while striving to establish our own identities within the classroom. In my experience, whether you are team teaching all day or for a period or two, the most successful situations evolve from mutual respect for the teaching abilities of those involved and the ability to collaborate to provide a quality educational experience for all of the students served. Successful educators working in team teaching situations embrace the teaching differences between themselves and their classroom partners. Each teacher has his or her own style, which should not be stifled by collaboration; rather, each style should be welcomed and respected as yet another way to reach every student. As professional educators, we must not be afraid of differing approaches or methodology and must be willing to learn from our most valuable and accessible assets, the teachers around us.

The motivation for any of us to take professional risks, strive for leadership roles, and think outside the box is the need to continually challenge and inspire our students. Through the concept of team teaching, students are consistently exposed to diverse teaching styles, differing personalities, and the chance to generalize skills taught between teachers. In my experience as the special education teacher in a team teaching situation, I have seen not only the students with disabilities blossom within the collaborative setting, but also the general education students as well. Through our efforts, the students that we serve have learned to accept different approaches within the classroom and have learned at a very early age that there are many authority figures in a school.

While I believe that team teaching and the collaboration that it involves is a beneficial situation for all parties, it takes a considerable amount of time and effort to make it successful. It is best when approached with an open mind and the goal of creating a successful learning environment for every student. Collaboration through sharing ideas and information, modeling new approaches, and communicating with all involved is the foundation on which a successful team teaching situation is based. Recognizing that each educator is an "expert" who brings different experiences to the classroom aids in the development of the idea that ownership is a team effort. With that, it becomes "our students," "our class," and "our success." Collaborative efforts within the classroom, school, or district lead to effective leadership at every level of the educational system.

In summary, whether you are already teaching in a team situation or considering the prospect, the following tips should be useful for creating a successful collaborative environment for staff and students alike.

Helpful Tips

- *Show Respect.* Respect the abilities, judgment, and contributions of your co-teacher. You will want the same in return.
- *Keep an Open Mind.* Embrace the differences in teaching styles and approaches.
- *Talk.* Keep the lines of communication open.
- *Stand Together.* Work through differences privately, and always present a united front to students.
- *Be Flexible.* Be willing to compromise.
- *Show, Don't Tell.* Lead by example.
- *Be Clear.* Expectations should be clear for all involved.

Using Staff Development to Implement a Schoolwide Reading Goal

Angela Judd
Hutchinson, Minnesota

Believing that all classroom teachers can and should teach reading strategies to their students, our school improvement committee at Hutchinson High School proposed the following goal: improve student reading scores on standardized tests, student reading comprehension, and student reading abilities. After presenting it to the staff, who endorsed the goal, a focused reading committee that included the media specialist was formed. We researched the latest data on reading programs and decided to introduce a limited number of initiatives each year and to focus on one schoolwide reading strategy during the first year.

To begin, I trained our staff in the KWL (What I *K*now, What I *W*ant to Know, and What I *L*earned) method the first year, encouraging teachers to use the pre-reading, during reading, and after reading strategies to help increase student understanding and achievement. Teachers were given laminated posters of the KWL chart for their classrooms. At the same time, we implemented the Scholastic Reading Program, encouraged all classroom teachers to participate, and provided training. We decided to have all the students take the Scholastic Reading Inventory test every year to provide us with comparison data. In addition, we designed an evaluation survey for teachers to use.

Since the Minnesota Comprehensive Assessment tenth-grade reading test used for the No Child Left Behind legislation asks mostly inferential/analytical and critical/evaluative questions, during the second year we added training in vocabulary strategies, and during the third year we concentrated on the types of questions to ask in the classroom. Using sample test questions and articles, I trained the staff in the differences between the types of questions as well as how to help students find answers in texts using the B+ (Is it an answer I can find if I go BACK in the text?) or H+ (Is it a method that I need to figure out in my HEAD?) method. That spring, all teachers wrote reading plans, indicating which methods they would use in their classrooms and how they would measure success. Teachers could choose KWL, Increasing

Inferential/Analytical and Critical/Evaluative Questions, Vocabulary Strategies, and/or the Scholastic Reading Program.

By the third year of our reading goal, over 3,000 books had been checked out of the library, compared to only 358 before we started the program. Not only had the number of books checked out grown dramatically, but the reading Lexile scores jumped as well. All grade levels demonstrated a decrease in the number of students scoring below grade level. At one grade level, almost half the students who had been reading below grade level improved their scores to grade level or above. In addition, the number of teachers using the program doubled.

This is our fourth year of the reading goal. I trained the teachers to use Reading Summaries and HUG (*H*ighlight the text, *U*nderline the details, and *G*loss/write notes on the margins). Staff members from 10 different departments currently participate in the Scholastic Reading Program, using it as required outside reading, extra credit, or supplementary reading. In the spring, teachers will meet during a staff development day to share the results of their reading plans, discuss their strategies, examine student work, and evaluate student achievement.

The media specialist and teachers report that students share excitement about reading, scoring 100% on their Scholastic Reading quizzes, and increasing Lexile scores. One ecstatic mother called the school counselor and told him how much her daughter was reading and that over the three years, she had increased her Lexile score from 772 to 1447. The average is 25 points a year.

Scores on the Minnesota Reading Basic Skills Test show improvement. For example, in the ninth and eleventh grades, the number of students passing in 2004 almost doubled compared to 2003. The Minnesota Comprehensive Assessment tenth-grade reading test results reflect that 81% of the students are at grade level or above. The scores in the Literal/Explicit, Interpretive/Analytical, Critical/Evaluation categories were all above the state average. On the state's School Report Card for our school, our reading proficiency rate was listed as 88.74%. These results validate our efforts.

One of the main reasons for the success of the goal was the focus upon one specific goal for four years and the use of staff development time to revisit the goal several times a year. Effective staff development centers on a school's instructional goals, is frequent and intensive, and includes follow-up exercises. If teachers reflect in an organized way, assess student work together, and share resources and strategies, a sense of collective responsibility for improvement of the school will build.

Helpful Tips

- Involve staff in writing the goal.
- Form a focused reading committee that includes the media specialist.
- Present research showing why all content teachers should teach reading strategies.
- Show the value of a schoolwide reading program such as Scholastic Reading.
- Focus upon one reading strategy in the beginning.
- Revisit the reading goal four times a year.
- Work on the goal for several years.
- Coordinate staff development time with the reading goal.
- Ask teachers to write individual reading implementation plans.
- Evaluate the success of the program and make necessary changes.

Statewide Teacher Training Networks

Angela Judd
Hutchinson, Minnesota

Often during staff development training teachers don't receive practical, hands-on materials that can be easily incorporated into a curriculum, or they don't receive information from a presenter who is currently teaching in the classroom. State education departments should use teachers for staff development training and offer opportunities for teachers to train other teachers throughout the state. The Minnesota Department of Education has a program called the Quality Teacher Network, which is a group of educators dedicated to assisting schools throughout

Minnesota to improve student achievement. I currently belong to the Language Arts QTN, which is organized and supported by the language arts specialist of the Division of Academic Standards and Professional Development in the Minnesota Department of Education. Our motto is "Improving Student Achievement Through Quality Teaching."

Network members are experienced educators who are selected on the basis of their content knowledge, pedagogical skill, leadership, and professional development experience. The networks are designed to represent the variety of schools and education professionals in Minnesota. The member selection criteria is as follows: administrative support; tenured evidence of investment in professional development (e.g., advanced degree, attendance at workshops/conferences, membership in professional organizations); evidence of leadership at school, district, region, state, or national levels; and diversity in grade levels, geographical location, gender, and school/district size. Each network also includes members knowledgeable about English Language Learners and Special Education.

QTN members receive professional development training. In return, QTN members provide services to their schools, other districts, and the Minnesota Department of Education. Services include training, mentoring, resource development, research, and advising. Delivery methods include workshops, study groups, mentoring, or working with curriculum teams. Members are expected to attend QTN professional development opportunities and provide evidence of engagement and service.

Our network offered several Summer Institutes in 2004 to teachers throughout the state. "Raising Writing Achievement in Secondary Students" and "Raising Writing Achievement in Elementary Students" gave teachers the opportunity to become members of a community of writers and teachers of writing who were focused on learning and practicing strategies that improve student writing. Another session, "Teaching Media Literacy and Research Strategies," helped teachers with the Minnesota Language Arts Standards that require students in Grades 3–12 to become critical users of information in print and electronic resources. This institute focused on strategies and tools that help students efficiently access, effectively process, and responsibly use information.

In the fall of 2004 and winter of 2005, another series of two-day workshops, titled "Raising Writing Achievement in Secondary Students through 6 Trait Strategies and Best Practices," was offered throughout the state. As a facilitator for these workshops, I felt that teachers appreciated the specific classroom experiences and materials that I could share about KWL, Minnesota's Language Arts Standards, Before/During/After Reading Instruction, RAFT (Role/Audience/Format/Topic) writing, Authentic Audiences and Purposes, Best Practices, the HUG Reading Strategy, the four types of writers, the Writing Process, Writing Summaries, Evaluation and Scoring, 6 Traits of Writing, and Examination of Student Work. Teachers especially appreciated practice in scoring student work. During one activity, teachers read student samples from the Minnesota Writing Basic Skills/Minnesota Comprehensive Assessment in Writing Exam and practiced scoring them. Another activity involved scoring student work using the 6 Traits. NWREL (Northwest Regional Educational Laboratory) has many student work examples on their Web site (http://www.nwrel.org). Valuable discussion occurred, and teachers agreed that they gained new insights as well as useful classroom materials.

It is invigorating to train other teachers. We meet as a group four times a year to share materials, work on projects, plan workshops, and read professional materials. The knowledge that I have gained by being a member of the QTN has been invaluable and the most useful professional development experience of my life.

Helpful Tips

- Always begin with an ice-breaking fun activity. One of my favorites is Penny for Your Thoughts. Ask teachers how many pennies they have handled in their lives. Then ask them to draw the front and back of the penny on a piece of paper. Next, pass out pennies for them to examine to check the accuracy of their drawings. Point out how we can be overly familiar with something and not really "see" it.
- Motivate teachers to listen by showing how this information will help them. Include professional research material to prove the value of your presentation.

- Provide a specific agenda and stick to it. Don't allow yourself to be sidetracked.
- Break the day into many activities. Keep each activity to no more than 45 minutes to ensure teacher interest.
- Use a variety of visual, auditory, and kinesthetic activities. Teachers as well as students have different learning styles. Have them journal, draw, perform, and play games like Jeopardy. Use the Carousel (where sheets are placed around the room and teachers circle the room, placing teacher-directed responses on each sheet) and the Gallery Walk (where teachers place ideas on sheets and walk around the room, looking at others' suggestions).
- Model best practices. Make the workshop a supportive setting for shared learning using active exchange and valuing ideas, collaborative small group work, and exercises.
- Keep a sense of humor and smile, smile, smile. If an issue arises, put it on a piece of paper called the Parking Lot, and tell the teacher that you will return to the problem later. Remember to return to the question later when the tension has decreased.
- Use Exit Slips and Entrance Slips for breaks or between days. Tell teachers in order to exit they must ask a question relating to the material learned on the slip. When teachers return, they must select one of the questions and answer it.
- Use fun quizzes with prizes to check for teacher understanding.
- Always end with an evaluation tool so that you may assess the success of the workshop. One of my favorites is the Square/Box/Circle Form. Have teachers write what "squares with their thinking" in the square, new ideas they've learned in the box, and questions they "still have circling" in the circle. Another favorite is the 3–2–1-Take Off. Teachers list "Something big I learned," "What I will do now (action I will take)," and "What I need (or want to know) next."

▧ Structured Freedom

Successful Schools Through Collaborative Learning Communities

Jason R. Harding
Monroeville, Pennsylvania

It takes a village to raise a child. Many great leaders have communicated these words of wisdom. They remind us that we can envision, implement, and achieve more when collaboration is a key factor in our everyday participation in society. In an age of standards and accountability, this premise could not be more appropriate and significant for educators. Collaboration is the key to success for all students. It is an essential ingredient in an educational environment that demands nothing less than that every student *can and will* learn in our classrooms. In order to develop this vision into reality, it will take much more than closing our doors to plan and teach on our own. We must build communities that are conducive to sharing ideas, knowledge, theories, and data collection. Only within these communities will our students be able to achieve at an optimum level in all instances, and will everyone reap the benefits of the experiences of those around them. We must openly communicate about what is working well and about areas in which we need to improve—in our instructional practices, individual student work, assessment results, and all components of student achievement.

You may be wondering, "How can I create this opportunity in my school?" The answer is found in a series of steps that will structure your freedom to communicate in an efficient, equal opportunity environment. This "Structured Freedom" cannot be achieved alone and will be a lifelong learning commitment. My goal is to provide you with a framework to create your own "Structured Freedom" promoting improved collaboration, data collection, and analysis with your colleagues. The process to create "Structured Freedom" is a long-term commitment that will take patience and dedication, but the result is well worth the effort.

1. Create a Vision Statement and Strategic Plan

If we want to know the path on which we will travel, we must first choose a destination. This is an opportunity as an educational leader to engage in a dialogue with the other members of your school community and develop a vision statement. The vision statement should encompass all that your collaborative school community will work to change, improve, and maintain over the course of the school year. All of your ships need to sail in the same direction in order for the process to be successful. If there are many areas that your collaborative school community decides need to be addressed, you should list all of them. The list should then be prioritized through collaborative efforts to analyze and discuss data presented by the group. Keep the items that are not at the top of the list, and implement them later as you begin to see progress in the higher priority areas. The high priority items will drive the strategic plan that is the foundation of your vision statement. The targets of the strategic plan should be measurable and achievable through the collaborative process.

2. Create Your Collaboration Pods

Now that you have created your collaborative community's vision and strategic plan, it is time to create the core groups that will make up the community. I call these your Collaboration Pods. Every collaborative learning community may choose to do this differently. Your Collaboration Pods should be made up of four to eight people. Some communities form the pods based on comfort level, some by balancing areas of expertise, whereas others just "count off by eights" and create their groups by chance. No matter which method you choose, the pod that you join will be your support group, your cheerleaders, your analysts, your confidantes, and the people you can count on when you have a problem. The problem may involve individual or group student work, teaching practices, or collaboration among a grade-level team. The Collaboration Pods will be the key to unlocking problem-solving strategies through discussion in a structured setting for your collaborative learning community.

3. Develop Data Collection Tools

We all have been exposed to data analysis and data-driven decision making due to the accountability that drives our education system today. Some educators view these terms as negative and not "student friendly" in their practice. Nothing could be further from the truth. If used correctly, data and the informed decisions that they can provide can forward student success. For this reason, data collection and analysis by your Collaborative Learning Pods are key factors for success. Before any presenters can begin to collect data to present their problem or student work to the Collaborative Learning Pod, the group must develop tools that will make the data collection practical and easily managed within a classroom. There are many options, ranging from a simple checklist to a more in-depth analysis with spreadsheets and graphs.

I believe that it is best to begin simply and to add to your "toolbox" as the Collaborative Learning Pod meets over time. The tools should fit the preference of each participant. The purpose is to ensure that each person feels comfortable and the rest of the Pod receives information and data that they can analyze for data-driven decision making. These options may get you started in building your own "toolbox":

  a. Checklists

  b. Tally Charts

  c. Rubrics

  d. Hand-Drawn Graphs

  e. Easy Grade Pro

  f. Excel Graphing/Spreadsheets

4. Develop Your Collaborative Learning Pod Expectations

Next, Pod members need to develop the structure that will allow everyone the freedom to teach and learn collaboratively. The Pod's expectations should help the group to be open and honest, enhancing the feeling that everyone is there to help and not to attack each other. The expectations should reflect everyone's feelings within the Pod.

This is an example of the expectations established by one of the Pods in which I participated:

a.   There will be one presenter and one facilitator at each meeting. The facilitator will ensure that the group sticks to the Pod's expectations. The facilitator should ask the Pod to refer to expectations 2–7 if anyone strays from them.

b.   The presenter will have 10 minutes to present his or her problem or student work to the rest of the Collaborative Learning Pod while everyone listens and takes notes. The presenter should present any data collection at this time for group analysis.

c.   The group should then use the data collection and information that the presenter has offered to them. The questions should be answered as they are asked individually. Once one question is answered by the presenter, it is not discussed in any way. The next question should follow and should be specific to the person asking it. It should not build on the question before it. This will eliminate the presenter feeling attacked by the other Pod members. The members should only ask one question until everyone has had an opportunity to question the presenter. Once this has occurred, members may ask a second question, a third question, and so on throughout the 10-minute time period.

d.   Then, the facilitator will have the group members discuss suggestions and possibilities for improvement for approximately 10 minutes. As they do this, the presenter will step back and take notes on the discussion. The presenter does not participate in the discussion and should not be addressed by the rest of the group. It is a reflective time for the presenter. The group members should avoid statements that attack and should use open language. This may include starting with "Based on the data, Joe could" or "I wonder if." These types of statements offer problem-solving strategies rather than try to solve Joe's problem for him.

e.   The facilitator should then ask the presenter to use notes to share what he or she has learned and how to implement this in the classroom.

f.   The Collaborative Learning Pod should then discuss what did and did not go well in the session.

g. The facilitator should remind everyone at the conclusion that all meetings are confidential in order to maintain the integrity and trust of the Collaborative Learning Pod.

5. Implement Ideas

Presenters take what they have learned and implement these suggestions in their classroom. Data collection should continue and the presenter should analyze the data regularly to see whether progress has been made. If it has, presenters should continue to collect data until they have reached their goal. Once they have reached their goal, they can begin collecting data in another area to present to the group the next time that it is their turn.

If the data show no significant progress, then the presenters should present the data along with another verbal description to the Collaborative Learning Pod to begin the process again. It is not a failure, only a speed bump on the road to success. The Pod should learn from the new data collected and why the previous recommendations were not successful for the presenter. This will open the door for even better, more informed data-driven decisions.

6. Different Environment Equals Different Processes

By now, some of you may be excited and ready to build a collaborative learning community. Others may be thinking that this is idealistic and will never work. We all are in educational environments, but they differ in demographic makeup. It is important that you take this basic process and make small changes to ensure success in your school. I cannot do this for you because you understand your current school environment better than anyone else.

I am fortunate to work for a large school district in an affluent suburban community in Pittsburgh. My resources and environment have helped me make this vision a reality more easily than it might in a school district that did not already have so much collaboration in place. This does not mean that it cannot be done. It means, instead, that an individual may have to work harder, develop the process at a different pace, find outside resources, or start with one small Collaborative

Learning Pod and build a collaborative community from the ground up. It does not matter how it happens or the length of time that it takes to do it. The common factor is that student achievement *can* increase through collaboration and all of society will benefit as a result.

▨ Lifelong Teaching and Learning

Linda Hodges
Fullerton, California

Many years ago, as a first-year teacher, I realized that the knowledge acquired during my college years was just a beginning; there was so much more I needed to learn about the subjects I was teaching. Almost 40 years later, I can honestly say that my efforts to learn more are still ongoing and what a joy it is. It inspires me!

Without a doubt, the best resources available to teachers are their colleagues. Interactions with other teachers as well as professionals from universities, business, and industry are invaluable. There is a vast array of opportunities for teachers to grow professionally through courses, workshops, conventions of professional organizations, and meeting with fellow teachers in their schools or districts.

As a teacher leader, one should keep abreast of educational developments and volunteer to serve on committees that examine school curricula and other policies such as school schedules and educational technologies that affect student learning. This will benefit your school and all the schools in your district, as it is important to have articulation among schools to ensure a proper scope and sequence in the curricula throughout the school district. Teacher leaders should work with administrators to foster cooperation among their schools.

Teacher leaders should set an example of professionalism through their own pursuit of means to improve their teaching. They must participate in as many professional growth opportunities as possible throughout the school year and during the summer vacation. Furthermore, they should encourage other teachers in their departments and schools to do the same. Most of the best teaching ideas are learned from other teachers. As a science teacher, I have been very fortunate because numerous companies, educational institutions, and government agencies (e.g., National Science Foundation) sponsor courses and programs for teachers. These sponsors include the University of California, Irvine; the Food and Drug Administration (FDA); Howard Hughes Medical Institute; Texas Instruments; The Jet Propulsion Laboratory; Chevron Corporation; The College Board; the Dolan DNA Learning Center; the Ocean Institute (Dana Point, CA); and the Northern California Society of American Foresters. A teacher has to look for these opportunities and take the time to apply for them and then attend them.

Using the resources gleaned from courses, workshops, and one's own teaching experience, teacher leaders can organize workshops of their own design to share ideas with other professionals. With the support and encouragement of my school administrators, I have had the privilege to foster professional growth in several ways:

■ Sharing expertise with teachers in my department and other departments in our school. For example, making computers and other technological instructional tools available to teachers and providing proper training for their use. Training is provided by experienced teachers from our school, workshops held at the county Department of Education, professional education conferences, and through companies specializing in educational technology.

■ Presenting workshops for teachers in other schools in our district or county. From contacts made at the University of California, Irving, I have presented workshops at several high schools and middle schools throughout the county and have demonstrated many science lessons for science workshops at UCI covering topics in genetics, biotechnology, and cell biology.

■ Conducting science workshops for elementary school teachers attending education conferences for the Diocese of Orange (my school district).

■ Inviting elementary, middle, and high school teachers to Saturday Science workshops held at my high school. Some of these workshops have been organized and presented by me; for example, a Food Science Workshop in 2003. Others have resulted from the collaboration of several teachers in our science department, all of whom are master teachers. A teacher leader recognizes the expertise of colleagues and welcomes their input whenever possible.

- Working with teachers from high schools and elementary schools in our district to articulate the curricular needs at all grade levels in an effort to improve the entire science curriculum and create an appropriate scope and sequence for the district.

- Coordinating a meeting of all science teachers from our district high schools. At this meeting, a keynote address regarding State Science Standards was given by a university chemistry professor who is very involved in state science education projects. This was followed by small-group sessions in which teachers shared ideas for teaching science.

As a department chair, I have spearheaded fundraising projects to support technology in my department and school. These funds have been used to purchase computers for the school computer labs as well as computers and other technology for science instruction such as calculators, DVD players, electrophoresis equipment, scientific probe ware to use with calculators and computers, projectors, spectrophotometers, video-flex cameras, and video-microscopes. Some schools have organized academic "booster clubs" of parents and community leaders who help with fundraising projects. Additional funding can be obtained through grants.

Teacher leaders enlist the expertise of community resources, recruiting outside professionals as guest speakers for classes, for school assemblies, or for faculty/staff enrichment. For example, speakers from the Audubon Society, Allergan Pharmaceutical Company, and a forensic anthropologist from a local university have addressed the students and faculty at our school. Field trips to local museums, universities, or educational centers should also be encouraged.

Finally, teacher leaders support a wide range of school functions, from athletics to theater and art projects, clubs, school publications, and service projects. It is important to show students that you care about them by your words and actions. Good teachers love what they do, recognize the gifts and talents of their colleagues, and learn from them.

Helpful Tips

- Seek dialogue with teachers and administrators in your school and with other schools.
- Encourage your colleagues to pursue professional growth opportunities.
- Raise funds for educational programs.
- Conduct workshops for other teachers.
- Support student activities.

Scopes Trial and Error

A Lesson in Integrated Teaching

Stacey Smiar
Cambridge, Massachusetts

Although we are a small school with small class sizes and combined grade levels, the crossover between the subjects is limited due to schedule and space constraints. Nonetheless, the social studies teacher, Jenn, and I, the science teacher, were strong believers in integrated learning and were determined to create at least one series of lessons that combined our two subjects. Jenn and I had already aligned our curriculum so that seventh and eighth graders were studying eugenics and the Holocaust while I was teaching genetics. Jenn's focus for the year was "Justice and Dissent," with one of her goals being to hold a mock trial in order to help students understand the justice system. She knew that I was interested in teaching Darwinism, so when she found a book on historic mock trials and came across the Scopes Monkey Trial, we knew we had found a perfect match.

For the social studies component, Jenn instructed students on how to perform a mock trial and research historic figures. As they read about

AUTHOR'S NOTE: Many thanks to Jennifer Kay Goodman for her collaboration with this article.

the controversy over evolution versus creationism, the kids were driven to gain a deeper understanding of the concept of evolution. After all, some of them were going to have to defend characters who believed in evolution, and some were going to have to argue that evolution was wrong. This is where science class took over, where we examined exactly what evolution *is*. What evidence is there? Who believes it and why? Who doesn't and why not? What does it mean to say that humans descended from monkeys? This brought us into a whole host of topics that I didn't plan and couldn't have predicted. Kids were fascinated by the various links and branches in the "family tree" of primal apes to Homo sapiens. We debated whether Neanderthals died off or mated with descendents of modern humans. We even hypothesized about the future evolution of human beings. What features would humans need? What wouldn't we need? How might the environment change, and how could we change the environment so we wouldn't have to change?

The result was a lively classroom full of twice as many students as usual. Student-made posters decorated the walls with sayings like, "Don't Make a Monkey Out of Me" and "Separation of Church and State." Students were focused on last-minute research and rehearsal of their characters. Having two teachers in the room helped us manage the energy of the room. The trial ensued with students acting out an historic conflict that incorporated more than just one discipline. We felt that students ended that unit with a much deeper understanding of both science and social studies and an improved ability to look at two sides of an issue.

I have had many experiences of working with colleagues on interdisciplinary teaching ideas. I've taught a sixth-grade interdisciplinary unit on the family farm and designed and led science research to help students understand the biomes and adaptations of various organisms in cultural studies they've done in social studies. In an effort to teach seventh graders research paper writing skills, an English teacher and I combined forces to create a project in which students would choose one of the human organs and write a research paper about it. In addition to teaching the students about the systems of the body, I also taught students how to responsibly research using the Internet, take notes, organize their ideas, and create a PowerPoint slide show. In a separate project, I worked with a math teacher on Excel spreadsheets and graphing to chart the growth of pea plants in science class. Also with sixth graders, the computer teacher and I worked together to teach kids to harvest images off the Internet and import them into a slide show to create a multimedia presentation of their "Breaking News Report" at a famous earthquake or volcano.

The common thread in all of these projects is that what existed at the start were a couple of teachers with enthusiasm and the hope that this could be a fun, different, and educational project. I've found what is most helpful is for the teachers involved to agree upon and clarify a goal at the start. Naturally you will plan some methods to reach the goal, but some will be figured out along the way; the kids' interests and stumbling blocks will help guide you.

As teachers, we put so much emphasis on kids working in groups, but rarely do teachers get the chance to do so. Working with another colleague, you have double the sense of each student's strengths and weaknesses. You learn more about each student both from your colleagues' different perspectives and from seeing the child in a different setting or working with a different skill. You grow as a teacher by challenging yourself with new curricula, new teaching methods, and new relationships with your teaching peers. The process is more time consuming than teaching and planning on your own, but it can be twice as rewarding.

Helpful Tips

- Clarify your goal. What skills or content do you want students to have at the end of your unit? This will keep you focused. For example, I knew when the students were writing about organs that I was to be most concerned with their research process and organization, *not* their acquired knowledge of the large intestine.
- Keeping your goal in mind, develop your means of assessment. Will students defend characters in a mock trial? Write a paper? Teach students of a younger grade?
- Establish your planning time. This is undoubtedly the most difficult part. You might pick a prep period during the week, meet before the school day starts, or agree that e-mail at

night works best for both of you. You will likely feel excited
and eager to have a colleague with whom you can debrief.

- If you can organize the time and space, there may be two
  teachers in the same room, or you may teach parallel
  lessons in your separate rooms. I feel it is more meaningful, if it is possible, for the students and teachers involved
  to come together at least at the culmination of the project,
  for both a sense of accomplishment and closure.
- Check your ego at the door. All teachers involved have to
  be willing to take risks, make mistakes, adapt to changes,
  and listen to their colleagues. You may not reach your goal
  as smoothly as you planned, but I haven't seen a collaborative project that didn't benefit the students in some way.
  And remember, you can try anything once, but you don't
  have to do it twice.

Staff Development Initiatives Within Faculty Groups

Scott Hogan
Phoenix, Arizona

As a graduation requirement, high school students in Arizona must pass
the Arizona Instrument to Measure Standards (AIMS) test by 2006 in
reading, writing, and mathematics. The April 2005 math test will have
approximately 100 multiple choice questions. As the AIMS Student
Guide puts it, "the questions will emphasize conceptual understanding, process, and problem solving skills rather than just computation
skills."[1] Students are not allowed to use calculators.

While most math teachers in our district know about the five
Arizona math standards (number sense, data analysis, algebra, geometry, and logic), district administration felt training was needed to help
teachers understand the different *types of math* on the test and *how to
cover* each kind of problem. Historically, our test scores have been very

low and clearly need to get better. Thus, we developed a workshop to address these issues. Three math teachers, Renae Short, Elaine Arrieta, and I, from different charter high schools in the Leona Group volunteered to present a workshop to math teachers from the district's other schools in a one-day format composed of two sessions, each running for close to an hour and a half.

We designed the math test preparation workshop in three distinct sections. The first section was titled "What Are the State Math Standards?" The second was "How to Cover Each Kind of Problem in Class," and the third we called "Roundtable Discussion of Strategies."

To prepare for the first part of the presentation, I downloaded the state math standards from the Arizona Department of Education (ADE) Web site and condensed the concepts within each standard into simpler language. I typed an example for each concept and used an enlarging machine at Kinko's to turn the 8 ½" × 11" pages into 18" × 24" posters. The copy was set to 26-point, black ink for maximum visual impact on the audience. At an office supply store I bought five three-packs of 20" × 30" foam board, a can of spray adhesive, and a utility knife to cut the foam board to size. I then mounted the enlarged copies onto the foam board. These 18" × 24" posters were the basis of my presentation. I explained each standard and the percentage each one was of the total test and also gave an example to illustrate each concept.[2]

The second part of the workshop involved going over the AIMS Practice Test published by ADE. Ordinarily the test's 43 sample questions are an integrated collection of problems that cover the five standards, in no special order. We decided to reformat the test; each problem was assigned a standard or concept and then placed in one of five categories that matched the state math standards (number sense, data analysis, algebra, geometry, logic). This grouping of practice problems by standard was the key to showing the types of math covered on the test. Each teacher was given two copies of the test, one an unedited version and the other with problem sets categorized by standards-based groups.

To further meet the twin objectives of the workshop, showing the types of math and kinds of problems covered on the test, we asked each teacher to bring a "curriculum map" of the classes he or she taught. A curriculum map, much like a road map for travel, lays out the essential topics of the course and covers skills, content, activities, and assessments used by the teacher. Such maps are useful tools to make sure you are on the right track, pacing yourself to teach the essentials. They can be fine-tuned to make sure your objectives are on target and students understand the concepts. We showed teachers a generic curriculum map, how to refine their initial curriculum draft, and how to use the map as a directional device for instruction.

The third section of the workshop was the roundtable discussion, in which we broke the audience into five-person groups. Each group had the large 3M Post-It notepaper to record strategies for covering each kind of problem on the test in the required math classes. The strategies recorded included giving each student a copy of the test formula reference sheet on cardstock the first week of on class; having students write answers on individual whiteboards instead of on paper; and giving all math tests in multiple choice format, similar to the AIMS test.

In summary, this three-part presentation was designed to help teachers understand the different types of math on the AIMS test and the importance of covering each kind of problem in classes that are required for our student population. In the process, standards and examples were presented on large posters, two kinds of practice tests were given to teachers, curriculum maps were used as tools for effective instruction, and a roundtable discussion allowed participants to share test preparation strategies.

This professional development workshop proved to be highly successful and offered a way for the math teachers in our district to come together to address an educational challenge. Renee, Elaine, and I worked together as the leaders on this project and found that collaborative leadership can lead to success for everyone involved.

Helpful Tip

Know how to use software, typed content, and foam board to create informative visual presentations.

Notes

1. Arizona Department of Education. (2004, September). *High school student guide to AIMS: Arizona's instrument to measure standards.* Phoenix, AZ: Author.

2. The percentages were obtained from Arizona Department of Education. (2005). *Spring 2004–2005 AIMS mathematics blueprint.* Phoenix, AZ: Author.

CHAPTER 2

Involving Community and Families

▨ Pioneer Days at Bowers Elementary School

Christopher R. Shadle
Massillon, Ohio

The third-grade students in our school have been studying communities
in their social studies curriculum. As part of this study, the students
examined communities of the past. The thematic unit covered a two-
month time period. In this unit, the children studied how our country
developed from the earliest settlements of the Native Americans,
explorers, colonists, and pioneers who settled in the Ohio Valley. The
children studied communities of the past in order to gain an appreciation of their heritage. Through integration and various learning channels, the pupils experienced learning the past through the "hands-on"
approach of learning by doing.

The students learned about the past communities through literature, costumed interpreters, videos, as well as hands-on learning activities. A wonderful part of the unit involved having the students compare communities of the past with communities of the present by visiting Schoenbrunn and Zoar, two historic sites in Ohio.

During their studies, the children wrote illustrated books about the way they envisioned life in the past. They were able to see the effort people put forth in order for our nation to develop. This experience developed the children's expository writing abilities in order to prepare them for the fourth-grade achievement tests. In addition, the children created a mural and used scenes from their books to illustrate a time-line of our country including the Native Americans, explorers, early colonists, and pioneers who settled here in Ohio.

The students learned how the pioneers as well as the Native Americans used natural resources in order to survive and to make products. The students hand-dipped candles from the natural resource of wax; they also made pottery candlestick holders for their candles. Each child had the opportunity to weave a scarf on a loom. This process gave the children an appreciation of the effort it took to make a finished product long ago. In addition, the children experienced a quilting bee as a pioneer "get together." Each student designed a square to illustrate his or her vision of pioneer life. All of the children helped sew the quilt together. In addition, a colonial auction was held where students described the purpose of each item. We discussed the economics of pioneer life including bartering, how people earned money, and the monetary system. Costumed interpreters shared the crafts that the early pioneers used when they first came to this country. Zoar interpreter Fred Wetshtein demonstrated the trade of the tinsmith. He made a tin lantern and a cup with the class. Zoar interpreter Nancy Ganyard demonstrated the craft of spinning as she discussed pioneer life in Ohio.

As a culminating activity, the children celebrated all the people from the past who helped to establish and develop our present community with a Pioneer Day that included a pioneer dinner. The first part of the day provided opportunities for the children to make log cabins, to make tin-punched decorations, to stencil, to paint with watercolors, and to write with quill pens. Parent volunteers assisted the children with the craft activities. This parent involvement was a great way to connect the students' homes with their school activities. Another parent designed and built a functional loom that would have been used in households of long ago. Students were given opportunities to weave on this classroom loom.

Prior to the pioneer dinner, a commemoration was held to remember and be thankful for everyone who helped develop our local community, our state, and our nation. Following the dinner, costumed interpreters described pioneer life and demonstrated the craft of spinning to the children and their families. The Pioneer Day was also a day for the children to display their work. Among items on display were the scarves they wove, the candlesticks they made, the candlestick holders they molded, the quilt they sewed, and the books they designed as well as a model of Schoenbrunn that they created together. The funds for this project were provided through grants from the National Educational Association and the Ohio Arts Council.

Using School/Community Partnerships to Teach History, Heroism, and Heritage

Deborah Forringer and Eileen Serene
Rural Valley, Pennsylvania

Never tell a twelve-year-old he is still a child. He thinks he knows more than you, and that is enough. A sixth grader already knows his parents are way behind the times and "uncool." Last year's and last week's studies and homework are long past, never to be needed again. Those things are ancient history, just like the old people and old stories in the social studies book. He is never going to get a chance to see any historical sites or visit any government buildings anyway.

Our students live in a very small, rural town in western Pennsylvania. They come from families that eke out their livings from an environment that has seen the closing of coal mines, the tearing down of steel mills, and the public auction of farmland. These same families, however, still retain their sense of pride and succeed in preserving their heritage.

The Pennsylvania State Assessment Standards require students to "comprehend historical events and their significance in a timeline order." A short lifetime of twelve or fewer years does not allow students to really put times past in perspective. Our first inspiration to add life and meaning to the social studies course came in 1999 from our state representative, Fred McIlhattan. Having close family ties with our community and faculty, he approached us with a project to help renovate and maintain a monument at the Gettysburg Battlefield. After gaining administrative approval, we approached our Parent Teacher Organization (PTO) for ideas and help with fundraising. To our delight, we were overwhelmed with their help and encouragement. We decided to center the entire school year's activities on the theme "Restore Our History." Pens with the theme imprinted were sold, and the PTO donated the profit from a pie sale to refurbish our chosen monument of the 62nd PA Infantry.

After careful research, we found that the men and boys of our area fought in this infantry, and many community members had pictures to show and stories to tell to our students. Having heard of our project, a local Civil War reenactment troop contacted us. They were invited to our school for an entire day of camp. Each grade of students rotated through different learning stations on the era's marching, weaponry, clothing, music, women's roles, food, battle geography, and soldier's life. The students researched chosen topics and wrote essays. The spring band concert program presented the most popular songs of the North and South.

In partnership with Representative McIlhattan, we decided that the best way to "live and experience" the Civil War was to actually see a battlefield. Gettysburg is only a four-and-a-half-hour drive from our school. He proposed that we apply for a state grant through the Pennsylvania Department of Community and Economic Development. We were awarded a grant of $5,000 for transportation, tour guides, admissions, and meals for our fifth- and sixth-grade students to see Gettysburg firsthand. With the direction of the guides, we reenacted Picket's Charge, "fired" cannons, retraced the strategic maneuvers of the troops, and found the 62nd PA Infantry Monument. Another Civil War reenactment troop from central Pennsylvania had read of our plans in a newspaper article and contacted us to ask whether they could meet our students at the battlefield to relate their stories. Plans were made to make the troop part of a ceremony in which three students would read winning essays at the monument, retell the known history of the 62nd PA Infantry, and record the event in pictures and video for future students. The students' history comprehension level of and changed attitude toward "old people and old stories" in social studies challenged us to continue with the teaching strategy of making their lessons come alive.

In the spring we chose a topic for the next school year, to give us time to organize our community resources and activities. Our citizens are blue-collar workers. Many are only second- or third-generation Americans working in coal mines, steel mills, factories, on farms, or at other manual labor. The era of the Industrial Revolution presented itself as our next course of study. Last year's fifth graders were now enthusiastic participants in researching background information. They led and encouraged the new class of fifth graders to research their genealogy, discover the occupations of their grand and great-grandparents, and discover family ethnic traditions. Family trees and research papers prepared the students for visits to the Johnstown Flood Museum and Johnstown Heritage Museum. These museums showed how industrial progress in factories, transportation, and communication both helped and hurt our area. The Heritage Museum provided each student with a card detailing the country of origin of an immigrant, his age, occupation, family unit, home environment, social status, and free time activities. The tour made the students take the role of immigrants and placed them in real-life situations. The students also visited the Pittsburgh Heinz History Museum to learn how the early industrial era directly affected the jobs their parents have today, and how the sports teams in Pittsburgh got their start.

All the music for the spring band concert was composed during the industrial era, and the songs were played in chronological order. Groups of students thoroughly researched each composition to compile a narration with program notes detailing the U.S. President at the time and major historical events that took place, such as inventions and states added to the union. The narrator and several participants were dressed in costumes of the era. The songs' subject matter covered railroads, bicycles built for two, a World's Fair, vaudeville, telephones, the Panama Canal, automobiles, Broadway, and sports. Baseball is a major sport in our area, and the band was invited to play "The Star-Spangled Banner" for a Pittsburgh Pirates baseball game at the brand new PNC

Park Stadium. A tour of the stadium included a lesson on the inception of the team; each factory or mill would field a team to compete for bragging rights.

In the fall of 2000 was the presidential election. Students learned of the popular and electoral voting process, then conducted mock elections. Sample ballots from the county courthouse made the process more official. We decided that the next year we would focus on the history of our armed services and our nation's wars during the twentieth century while "Honoring All Who Served."

Our community has a very large number of veterans. Many American Legion members had been assisting us for years with our Veterans Day assemblies; they were continually searching for ways to assist us in our classrooms. Plans were made for our students to survey our community to compile names of all the living veterans and document their biographies and experiences in a published booklet. This booklet would be given to each family represented in our school, all veterans included in the book, and the library. Fall 2001 saw our plans well in order and underway. We had applied for a grant from the SHOPPA Foundation and received $1,000 to publish our booklet.

Another Community and Economic Development grant of $5,000 was to be used to take our students to Harrisburg to tour the state capitol building. Then the tragedy of September 11, 2001 struck. Our plans for honoring those in uniform took on greater meaning. A student initiated a drive to collect supplies needed for the clean up in New York at Ground Zero. Plans for the Veterans Day assembly were expanded to include a guest speaker to talk to the students on the importance of serving their country. Our students wrote essays on "What It Means to be a Veteran." The winning essays were read at the assembly and the authors were presented with flags by the American Legion. The Legion provided a full color guard for the Pledge of Allegiance, the singing of the national anthem, and the playing of "Taps." Students began to canvas the neighborhood for biographies of our veterans.

The stack of entries came in at an incredible rate. We knew the community had a large number of veterans, but the actual number was staggering. A fresh patriotic fervor had permeated our community. We discovered that many of our students' parents were currently in the military. After some of the older veterans were interviewed, they called the school to thank us for taking on such an endeavor; they liked being recognized and appreciated after all the many years. The students had to sort the entries by branch of service and the war, conflict, or peacetime service in which each veteran had been enlisted. The World Wars and conflicts were being taught in social studies classes. As the time for our anticipated trip to Harrisburg drew near, the administration, teachers, and parents expressed concern as to the advisability and safety of visiting a public government building. After much consideration, it was decided to forgo the trip to Harrisburg. The entire Community and Economic Development Grant of $5,000 was returned to the state. If we could not go out of the building, then we would provide opportunities for veterans to come to us.

Effort was made to obtain a military band to give a concert for our elementary and high school. Due to the Homeland Safety alert and the short notice, no military band could comply. Our elementary band then planned a concert of patriot music, which included all the military anthems and hymns. The ambulatory patients from a nearby veterans' hospital were invited to come speak to our students and then were treated to a luncheon and a matinee of the band concert. All veterans whose biographies were published in the booklet were also invited to the concert, and everyone stayed for an All-American Apple Pie Reception.

By meeting and talking with these proud veterans, our students gained respect for the men and women who had sacrificed so much. Liberty, freedom, service, dedication, and sacrifice were now tangible elements in the students' young lives. The veterans also donated military uniforms, ribbons and medals, pictures, and equipment to display in the school's showcase for all the students to see and study. To help honor and remember these loyal men and women, we designed a bronze plaque engraved with our theme "Honoring All Who Served," placed it on a white marble stone, and placed it in front of our school by the flagpole for all to see. Our school custodian, who was the commander of the local American Legion, obtained flag-holding markers of all the wars and conflicts to display around the plaque. The sixth graders assisted the American Legion with placing these military markers on veterans' graves in a local cemetery for Memorial Day.

The events of the September 11, 2001 disaster still had an effect on our plans for the 2002–2003 school year. Many community organizations had gone to New York to lend aid and donate supplies. Our students needed to learn about citizenship. They needed to learn the historical development of the fire and police departments. They needed to know about the jobs of the people in the public service sector, the astronauts who explored the frontiers of space, and the local government officials who kept their community running smoothly. They needed to be "Saluting Everyday Heroes."

A commemorative ceremony was held at the flagpole on September 11, 2002 to remember those who perished and those who provided aid. An aide to President Bush had heard of our school's special programs, assemblies, and efforts to teach the students history, honor, and patriotism. He gave our school a wreath titled "The American Spirit in All of Us" made with the wheat from the plane crash site in Shanksville, only an hour south of our town. The President sent an autographed photo and message congratulating our school. The students were made aware that heroes come from all walks of life. They would be learning of the historical heroes in the social studies book, but heroes lived among them every day.

Researching and writing essays on past heroes was now an easy chore. The fundamentals of note organization, outlining, and drafting the composition were clearly understood. A Veterans Day assembly featured some of these essays, with the winners receiving flags from the American Legion. This had become a tradition much anticipated by both the students and the Legion. Our guest speaker was a young, newly elected state representative from a neighboring district who was also a veteran. He enumerated the hometown heroes the students might encounter any day on the street. The students were challenged to be heroes themselves by learning to be model citizens. This would include comporting oneself in a way younger students could emulate, learning the functions of government and society to become a good citizen, helping others when possible, and always taking the opportunity to thank someone who has helped you or served our country in any way.

Our PTO arranged a career day for the students. Community members representing many facets of employment explained their jobs and the qualifications needed to obtain them. Participating were mining executives, nurses, doctors, prison wardens, farmers, firefighters, and politicians. The band's spring concert featured a salute to the Challenger Space Shuttle and a bagpiper to help with the playing of "Amazing Grace." The students learned that this hymn was used to honor fallen police officers and firefighters.

During the summer of 2003, we were chosen to attend the Teach Vietnam Teachers Conference in Washington, D.C., sponsored by the Vietnam Veterans Memorial Fund. We attended four days of clinics, classes, and lectures on ways to teach our students about this controversial time in our nation's history. We listened to best-selling authors, saw videos of documentaries, read articles of fact and fiction, and saw examples of other teachers' lesson plans and projects. We attended a breakfast with our senators and representatives in the Capitol building, toured historical sites, and participated in a moving closing ceremony at the Vietnam Veterans Memorial where each of us honored a fallen Vietnam veteran of special importance to us.

Each year we had used the local resources available to us to bring history alive for our students. It was impossible to take our students to Washington, D.C. to see the Wall or tour the sights. But was it possible to bring the Wall to us? Application was made to the Vietnam Veterans Memorial Fund to have The Wall That Heals come to our community. The exhibit included a one-third size replica of the memorial and a museum with chronological history, showcases of memorabilia, and computerized information about all the names engraved on the Wall. One of the compelling reasons to bring the Wall to our community was the fact that 30 names from our county appeared on it, several of those being from our small town. Circumstances of grief, age, and opportunity had prevented immediate family members from visiting the memorial in Washington, D.C. Only two of our school's students had ever been to our nation's capital. The information detailing the cost of the exhibit, the fees for the caretakers who traveled with it, and the specifications for its display were mind boggling. There was usually a two-year waiting list for available dates. We approached the administration and PTO to see if the crazy idea was at all possible. They gave us a confident approval. While waiting for response to our application and researching funding possibilities, we again held the annual Veterans Day assembly with an emphasis on remembering our Vietnam veterans. An

American Legion member and Marine veteran was the father of one of the veterans we honored at the ceremony in Washington, D.C. A rubbing of the son's name from the memorial was presented to the father. Rubbings of all the names on the Wall from our county, Vietnam-era military memorabilia, equipment, and uniforms from the community were displayed in the school's showcase. The guest speaker was a Vietnam veteran who was still on active duty in the Reserves and expected to be called to Iraq at any time.

A reply to our application to host The Wall That Heals came in January; our dates were in April on Easter weekend. The school board would never approve those days, and it would still be snowing in western Pennsylvania at that time. Innumerable communications with the scheduling organizers finally provided us with a date in May. Getting funding was the next big step. In partnership with State Representative Fred McIlhattan, we searched for funding to bring the Wall to our community. He paved the way for us to receive another $5,000 state grant from Community and Economic Development and $500 from the Pennsylvania State Education Association. Donations came from our school district's Educational Foundation, the PTO, county commissioners, American Legions, Veterans of Foreign Wars organizations, insurance companies, the Business and Professional Women's Organization, the William Penn Association, the town borough council, and private citizens. The local American Legion spearheaded the scheduling of volunteers needed for 24-hour security during the five days' visit of the Wall; every Legion and VFW in the county participated. The community park was chosen as the location to display the Wall and its museum. Community volunteers were on hand to assemble the Wall on the Wednesday evening it arrived. The local community television station and newspaper, along with the major television networks from Pittsburgh, covered the events.

Our school board and administration had given permission for all 2,000 students in our school district to visit the exhibition. Each day started with a solemn opening ceremony with every American Legion and VFW in the county participating. School officials and veterans delivered speeches; high school choirs from our school district sang "The Star-Spangled Banner" and other selections. The elementary band presented a concert of patriotic music. An American flag that had flown over the state Capitol and a state flag that had flown in Vietnam during the conflict were presented to us and flown during the visit.

Saturday was Community Day. The Rolling Thunder motorcycle veterans visited and politicians delivered speeches. Each day community members read the list of names of the local casualties engraved on the Wall. Many people left tributes at the Wall in memory of loved ones. The high school Leo Club, sponsored by the Lions Club, assisted visitors with locating names on the Wall and collected the tributes daily, tagged them for identification, and later displayed them at the school.

Sunday was Mother's Day. The culminating activities began at noon with all the town church bells ringing, followed by an ecumenical church service led by community clergy. High school students sang solos, and a rose was placed at the Wall for each local casualty. We had arranged a flyover of C130 cargo planes but were informed by the Pentagon that the unit had been called to Iraq. We received a SHOPPA Foundation grant to purchase disposable digital cameras that the students used to make pictorial documentaries of the event. A video documentary was also filmed to use with future students. A commemorative bronze plaque was designed and placed at the park so all would remember the visit of the Wall to our community.

Helpful Tips

- Establish a close professional relationship with administrators.
- Incorporate technology to teach, research, and promote learning activities.
- Contact and visit local community and service organizations that can be used as resources in the classroom.
- Search publications and Web sites for grant opportunities to fund classroom projects.
- Actively participate in your school's Parent Teacher Organization.
- Survey parents and community members for volunteers or teaching resources.
- Form educational partnerships with the government and business people in your area.

- Plan with fellow teachers to coordinate an interactive and integrated course of study.
- Be flexible; plans always have a way of changing, but don't give up.
- Utilize the news media; publicizing your plans and projects often results in additional volunteers and funding.
- Students are sometimes the best source of ideas; leave room in your plans for their growth and input.
- Document everything in writing, pictures, or video; you will forget.
- Use past projects to teach future students.

▧ Finding Your Lost Dutchman Mine

Dennis Griner
Palouse, Washington

It is the late 1800s. Jacob Walz is just emerging from the foothills of the Superstition Mountains range south of Phoenix. His heavily laden mule struggles under the weight of the gold ore in the saddle packs. This trip is like the many other trips Walz has made, but with one exception: this trip will be his last. He will die in 1891 of poor health with a sack of gold under his bed. To this day, people from all walks of life are drawn to the Arizona desert to search for the elusive Lost Dutchman mine and the fabulous riches there—the fabulous riches waiting just for them.

This short story provides us insight into human nature while providing a framework to discuss an important educational issue. For educators, too, there is an ongoing search for riches. These riches are not those found in a pay raise (although that would be nice), nor are they found in a gold mine. The riches educators seek are in the form of parent and community involvement in the classroom. These are our figurative gold mines. Unfortunately, for many educators this treasure is as elusive as the Lost Dutchman mine. They have worked hard for years to find it. They have heard stories of others having hit it rich, but their personal hunt has left them disappointed. Dedicated teachers, however, are as determined in their search for their gold as those in Arizona. They do not give up on the dream. They do not become disheartened. They continue their hunt.

I am one of the fortunate ones. I have found the treasure. I have parental and community support for my program. The difference between my story and the story of Jacob Walz is the fact that I will provide the map I used to get there. I will be honest and up front on this issue. Like hunting for gold, getting parental and community involvement in your classroom takes long hours of hard work and many disappointing moments along the way. However, in the end when your goal is achieved, it will be worth it all.

I began teaching in 1972 in the rural logging community of Deary, Idaho. From my first day of class, I had the desire to motivate my students to think outside the four walls of the classroom. When I introduced a new unit, I knew I had to get past my students' "how will I ever use this" attitude. I chose to apply the academics of the classroom to the world they knew. I sought out local foresters to teach how to apply their math skills in the woods by determining the height of trees and learning to tell the history of a tree's life, as well as its age. My students learned how to take a core sample of a living tree and "read" the information it contained. To learn Native American culture, we attended Pow Wows to taste the food, learn the dances, and study the history and culture of the people. My students studied the impact of logging and the environmental issues it raised by asking local leaders to speak in class. There were valuable lessons in the field trips to the woods and local mills to learn from the workers how industrialization was changing the lives of their families. Experts from many fields came to share their knowledge with my students. I began to create a resource file of local people who were effective speakers. My resource file grew and grew.

Very early on, I realized I was overlooking a major resource, family and friends of my students. It was about this time that I started my oral history units. It allowed all parents and extended family members to feel a part of the learning process for my students. It has been one of my most rewarding units in that students strengthen their connection to their families and families strengthen their connection to the school. Designing a unit of oral history or a similar unit that involves family is a major step in accomplishing that home-school connection.

When I moved to my present district 23 years ago, I brought with me my bag of tricks. I have since expanded and modified this to fit the rural, farming community of Palouse, Washington. Now we study farm-related issues such as water rights, pesticides, fertilizers, dams on the river, and world markets for grain. The setting has changed, but the approach has stayed the same. To be truly successful in parent and community support you must bring the community into your classroom and take your classroom into the community. You must reach out. For me, using multimedia has proven to be a successful approach.

I developed a television broadcasting class in our high school over a 15-year period. (Remember I said it might take long hours and hard work.) The program has evolved into running the two educational channels from my classroom. My students broadcast live sporting events, concerts, and other special events to the community as well. I know what you're thinking at this point—big budget, large school; wrong on both accounts. We have a high school student body of just over one hundred students in grades 9 through 12. Community and parental support built over time has made this possible.

Your project does not have to be that ambitious; it just needs to be sincere and address the needs of your students and the community. The formula for success is simple: find a need in your community and help your students meet it. Another example may help; my students provide the extra hands for Haunted Palouse, a three-day event for Halloween. Our business association and city council sponsors this event, which promotes our community and provides a safe and fun Halloween for children. The event is nothing out of the ordinary, yet my students' willingness to work in the community does not go unnoticed. If you want to gain parental and community support, you need to seek out similar service opportunities. By becoming involved, you make the connections that will promote your program in the community while strengthening the ties between families and school.

There is a saying among miners, "Gold is where you find it." This statement has a ring of truth, but dedicated teachers know that personal vision, hard work, and commitment are also essential ingredients. My map to success I pass on to you: bring family and community members into the classroom, and get your students involved in the community. Your own personal Lost Dutchman mine is within your grasp.

❦   The Three "Cs" in Education

A Classroom, a Community, and Collaboration

Erica Drennan
Red House, West Virginia

The teaching profession encompasses many roles, including roles that go outside and beyond the classroom. To many, teaching may appear to be a profession that involves standing in front of the class for several hours each day and teaching the students to solve math problems, read, and write. Fortunately, the teaching profession is so much more than the way it is perceived by some people. Not only do teachers teach all of the academic subjects, they must find ways to provide exciting and motivating lessons and involve family members in the education of the students. Teachers fulfill many roles, and one important role is leading and participating in parent and community outreach initiatives.

Involving family and community members can pose many challenges for teachers. The first challenge is remembering to involve these members in our instructional day. As effective teachers should, we tend to focus on the students and how to teach them the important concepts of each academic area. Students are the main priority and the attention is given to them. Often, teachers forget to involve other members outside the classroom in the learning process. Another challenge that we face is trying to motivate some family and community members to become involved in the learning process. Often, we find it difficult to have parents even help the students with their homework. It can become very discouraging. Beyond this challenge is the challenge of finding ways and managing instructional time to allow the family members and community members to become involved.

In an attempt to overcome the above-mentioned challenges, we must activate our creativity. When planning lessons, it is important to look at what is being taught and search for ways that others can be involved. For example, when planning a reading lesson, have a parent or another community member come into the classroom to read the story that goes along with the lesson. If the story is about a particular animal, a community member could visit the classroom and talk about and show the animal.

Although the teacher plays the primary leadership role in the classroom, it does not mean that others cannot help teach the lesson. Community members have a wide range of knowledge and can share what they know about many concepts in science, history, other countries, other cultures, and so on. Talk to parents of your students and allow them to help you find the resources that are needed. With the cooperation of others, the challenge of finding ways that family and community members can become involved seems a little less overwhelming.

Often, we find ourselves in a situation where we want to involve others in the learning process but are discouraged by the lack of response. Fortunately, from firsthand experience I know there are always at least a few parents who want to be involved. Take advantage of those parents first, and use them in any way possible. To motivate others, it seems to help if they are involved from the beginning. Be sure to send home weekly newsletters about what is happening in the classroom. This allows the family members to feel like they know what is going on at school. Always be appreciative and send thank you notes when others do become involved in the classroom. Find a topic of interest that is within the "comfort zone" of a family or community member and he or she may be more willing to participate. Often, lack of involvement could be due to lack of knowledge in a particular area. If members do not want to come to the school, find possible field trip ideas that correlate with the curriculum and take the students out into the community. Motivating others to become involved can become discouraging at times, but it is important not to give up on the idea.

Helpful Tips

Ideas for Getting Others Involved

- Send home weekly newsletters.
- Have students write cards to community members who are facing a difficult situation. (Great writing activity!)
- Read aloud.

(Continued)

(Continued)

- Do a holiday craft.
- Teach about another culture or language, (e.g., Christmas Around The World).
- Teach about animals and bring animals to the classroom.
- Build a greenhouse (have community members help with the project) and donate plants to the community.
- Have students perform a play or puppet show as a culminating project to a reading story or a unit, and invite family members to watch.
- Organize field trips.
- Have students send postcards to family members about something happening in the classroom.
- Organize fundraisers for the school.
- Learning centers; have a center that a parent can lead.
- Help with computers; this is particularly useful for elementary students who are not able to use a computer independently yet.
- Have a parent or community night and have students showcase their work.

Getting Started With Volunteers

- Send out a survey at the beginning of the year asking parents how they would like to become involved in the classroom.
- Be clear about your expectations when involving others in the learning process. If not, the parent may decide to stay in your classroom all day.
- Make it known that it is still your class, and don't let others just take over.
- Be sure that students know that the classroom rules do not change, even when a parent is in the classroom.
- Make the family/community members feel welcome. Possibly send a postcard letting them know that you're excited about them coming.
- Always be sure to send a thank you note as a follow up.

▨ Parent Involvement

Jessica Galla
Cumberland, Rhode Island

I believe one of the key elements of a successful year is communication with parents. As teachers, we have the children 6.5 hours a day. This is a long time for children to be away from home. It would be very beneficial if parents knew what the children were learning in the classroom during this block of time each day so they could be reinforcing the key concepts at home as well. Schools have high expectations for children, and if parents are reinforcing those expectations at home, a child's knowledge can only improve.

Children often have a difficult time trying to explain to their parents what they do in school. A typical response to the question, "What you did in school today?" is, "Nothing" or "Stuff." It is often hard or overwhelming for a young child to explain his or her day. It is much easier if the teacher and parent have direct communication. To help with this, last year I started using a Web site called SchoolNotes (www.schoolnotes.com).

SchoolNotes is a free Web site for teachers to communicate with parents and students, and I have found it to be a very valuable tool. In fact, I wish I had known about this Web site earlier. Many parents last year thanked me for using the Web site. I update my page every Sunday night with the lessons for the week. I add the key concepts for each subject. I also put daily homework assignments on the site. I teach first grade, and often the children "forget" what the homework assignment is. This page is a way for the parents to know ahead of time what is expected for the week.

At the beginning of the school year, I send home a letter stating that I use the Web site. I offer parents a printed version of the weekly page if they prefer that (or for those who do not have a computer). I pass out the printed version on Monday morning. Parents also have the option to sign up to be electronically notified when I make any changes to the page. I have to say the majority of the parents in my classroom have signed up for this notification system. To date, I have not had any negative comments about using SchoolNotes.

One thing you need to consider before you use the Web site is that you need to update it regularly. If you are going to use it and be enthusiastic about it at the beginning of the school year but aren't able to maintain it throughout the year, I suggest not using it at all. The parents come to rely on the site, and they would be very disappointed if you stopped using it.

Parents are also able to e-mail you using SchoolNotes. The e-mail goes directly to your home e-mail but the parents don't have access to that address. I believe it is easier for some parents to e-mail instead of writing a note or calling. I receive many e-mails from parents each week. I'm glad that they feel comfortable enough to ask questions about their children and ways to help them at home. The parents in my classroom know that I will get back to them the next day, if not the same day. I believe that educating parents about what is being taught in the classroom is important. In addition to SchoolNotes, I also use parent volunteers.

When I first started teaching I was a little apprehensive about having parent volunteers come into the classroom. I thought they were there to watch me. That really isn't the case in most instances. Last year, I had a parent volunteer come to our classroom each day. The parents want to help the children. In most cases they don't want to watch me. The children are aware that the parents are taking an interest in their education. As long as the children can handle their parents coming in, I believe it's a great idea.

Finally, I have found that parents contribute to their children's education in different ways. Last year, a colleague and I had an "Animal Habitat Museum." We were working on animal habitat projects, and we wanted to have a "showing" of our projects for the parents and relatives. When we opened our doors to them, we could not believe how many parents and relatives came to see our classes' projects. The parents went around our "Museum" and asked the children about their animals and their habitats. For the most part, the children were very knowledgeable about their animals. I think it's very helpful to involve the parents in their child's education as much as possible. They may have helped the child with the research, the presentation, or report. Parents like to see the final product of their children's work. So whether you contact them electronically, have them in as volunteers, or offer "project-sharing times" like our Animal Habitat Museum, invite parents into your classroom!

▧ Let's Take It Outside

Creating a Community Learning Environment

Linda Keteyian
Detroit, Michigan

As a young teacher, I was quite convinced that I could take on the world (including my classroom) single-handedly. I would be inspiring, thoughtful, and prepared. My students would adore me and go on to do great things. Many teachers will recognize my self-important naïveté as well as the humbling experience that was my first year. June of 1984 saw me exhausted, determined, and armed with the little epiphany that has driven my teaching ever since. Not only can I *not* teach alone, I was never meant to. Helping a child grow into a well-balanced, intelligent adult who uses his or her powers for good takes an entire community of which I am only a small part. The teachers in my building who complained the most were also the most "independent," the least willing to work on school projects with a team, and the first to point out the shortcomings of others or the potential problems of any programs we might want to implement. The idea of working with a parent or community member horrified them: What did these people know about education? Our job was hard enough without including them. I was faced with the choice of following in their well-worn footsteps or seeking out a different kind of mentor. One of my favorite scientists, Margaret Mead, once wrote, "Never doubt that a small group of thoughtful, committed citizens can change the world. Indeed, that is the only thing that ever does." I knew that if I wanted to see changes in my classroom, my teaching, and my students, I would have to begin taking a leadership role in creating that change.

In keeping with the spirit of Mead's admonition, I began to look for school projects that suited my skills. I had begun a science club that dabbled in after school programs, and they were interested in helping out in the school community. We took a look around and decided a general school cleanup was in order. Our first effort was heartfelt but not well attended. We had three teachers, one parent, and seven children. It was hardly a "schoolwide" event. Since then I have taken great care to plan well in advance and organize activities in a way that attracts as many groups as possible. We began to work with Volunteer Impact, a group that involves many of the local businesses. We also use flyers and newsletters to keep our families well aware of what is going on and how they can help. We now have several annual activities that are well attended. Our first event of every school year is Clean Up Day, which takes place in the fall. The school families spruce up the gardens (all planted by the science club with help from The Greening of Detroit), paint over any lockers that need it, and give the school a general once over. Parents like to help out because they have a good deal of input into what we do and how it is done. They also use this opportunity to suggest any changes we can make to the school grounds.

Additional annual events include our planting at the Springwell Post Office and the Fourth of July parade. Our children chose the Post Office because they pass it regularly and the front of the building had a barren section of dirt. We wanted to make it look better, so we enlisted the help of Southwest Detroit Environmental Vision. They supply the flowers and a little additional manpower, and every summer we enjoy the fruits of our labor each time we mail a letter. During the Fourth of July parade, our students follow behind with bags and pick up the trash people leave. The crowd loves to see us coming and will often hang on to their trash and give it to us rather than throw it on the ground as they have done in the past. We have had many comments regarding the good example our children are setting for the adults in the community.

With each project our school becomes a little more cohesive in its teaching practices. The parent group has begun to seek out the science club when it wants to plan an event. Teachers have come to me with ideas for school plays, field trips, and parent nights. Recently a third grader stopped me in the hall and demanded to know when I was starting a cheerleading club. When I told her I don't do cheerleading, she responded, "Well, the gym teacher says you should." I was somewhat taken aback until I realized that it was generally accepted that I would be willing to take on a project if the students showed an interest. Unfortunately, I don't do cheerleading (I draw the line at activities that require jumping), but the point had been made. Working as a team, including with parents and community members, is far preferable and certainly more effective than going it alone. The proof has been in the children's achievements.

Student learning has been impacted by each and every one of our community improvement activities. Students have learned how to identify a problem, where once they would have accepted what they saw as unchangeable. They have learned to come up with creative ways to address the problems they see, including deciding we needed a mural to cover the writing on the playground wall. When one of our students was concerned about an abandoned building and illegal dumpsite near her home, the children asked SDEV for help. They helped us organize a cleanup that included the removal of the building. The student was able to participate in the cleaning, and a camera was placed at the location to catch any future offenders. Teamwork is already a part of their thinking. They know they are members of a community that requires cooperation on the part of each and every member. Parents expect to be tapped as resources and community organizations know us by name and seek us out when they want to volunteer.

Recognizing the global nature of educating our children has provided the children the opportunity to take their education into their own hands and act as leaders in the community. It has given parents input they had been denied, creating a more positive relationship with the school. It provides the greater community a chance to give back and act as stewards for the environment and the children who live there. No one is left in doubt as to his or her contribution to each child's education or his or her role in creating a positive change in the world.

Effective Parent Involvement in the Classroom

Roxie R. Albrecht
Sioux Falls, South Dakota

The National Board for Professional Teaching Standards recognizes the importance of family involvement in their standards for each certificate area, as well as in the Five Core Propositions. Core Proposition 5 states "Teachers are Members of Learning Communities." This encompasses professional development and collaboration with colleagues, business partners, and families. It is the critical family connection that I am going to share with you.

When I first started teaching 30 years ago, family involvement was limited to parent-teacher conferences, attendance at programs and PTA meetings, and meetings the principal called with parents to discuss a child's infraction of a school policy.

Today my classroom has a revolving door of parents, grandparents, business mentors, and community resource personnel who are regularly invited to enrich the experiences of my 29 second graders. For parents unable to devote time to the regular classroom day, I have designed activities that allow them to be involved in their child's school experience in other ways (and beyond helping a child finish incomplete work from her school day).

Parent involvement in my classroom has evolved as I collaborate with others and seek out ideas that might enhance my own practice. The following activities have helped me involve parents who cannot come into the classroom on a regular basis (if at all). Their support is critical and highly valued through the opportunities I use to give them the opportunity to be integral partners in their child's school experience.

Before-the-Year-Starts Letter

In the National Standards for Parent/Family Involvement, communication is the first standard.

> Communication is the foundation of a solid partnership. When parents and educators communicate effectively, positive relationships develop, problems are more easily solved, and students make greater progress.

I begin communicating with families of my students before school starts; I send out a preschool letter and questionnaire. My purpose for this is twofold. First, I introduce myself and tell them a little about me. Second, I invite parents to tell me about their child. For example, one of the questions asks parents about areas of school life the child has especially enjoyed. I have found this information invaluable in beginning my school year. The first year I tried it, I felt like I knew the students as well as I would have by the first conference.

When asked or given the opportunity, parents share valuable insight into their child's abilities, attitudes, and areas of concern. This helps me immediately gain an understanding of the child I will be involved with. Parents are more than willing to tell you everything about their child. Research findings on parent involvement show greater achievement from higher grades and test scores, better attendance, and more consistently complete homework.

Through this invitation, I send a message that I welcome and value parent input and perspective. It sets the tone for the rest of the year. Parents are given time to reflect and think through their answers and to do it at a convenient time for them. Parents tend to be very open when writing. They tell the positive as well as the areas of concern. The questionnaire asks them to reflect on changes that have occurred in the child's life during the summer. It is here parents share life changes like divorce and death. They share physical changes and social changes. Parents are asked to write about areas of school the child has especially enjoyed. This helps me plan activities to "hook" the child right away. When parents address the question on special needs, they give me insight into their child's academic, social, or personal life. I ask parents what goals they have for their child this year. In general, parents have been very reasonable regarding their expectations for the year. They know their children, and when asked, share that information openly. The last question is totally open. "What else would you like me to know about your child or about you?" Invariably, the answer to this question is the longest and often the most helpful. I start my school year a step ahead of the students in my class. While 29 questionnaires are more than I can commit to memory, I have them on file and reread them periodically.

Student learning is directly impacted when I know up front which children have issues with reading or math. I know who needs help in developing positive friendships and who might need an extra hug. Parents share information on the questionnaire that I wouldn't find on a cumulative record, yet is so important in planning the first days and weeks of school. I know which child needs extra help in reading directions. I can position myself close to that child and track the lines of print as we read together. When students go home the first day, I want them to feel successful and that they have what it takes to accomplish the tasks in second grade. Scaffolding what they already know with small bites of new information is doable. The questionnaire helps me know where my scaffolding should begin to build, each child at his own level.

Parents as Classroom Volunteers

Each year at the Preschool Open House, I enlist the help of parents in the classroom. While I ask for a weekly commitment, I also encourage parents to give whatever time they can to our classroom activities. They can come in when they can find the time, and I will use their services. For example, a parent with multiple sclerosis has come in a number of times on days that she is feeling well. While she cannot make a regular commitment, she likes to be able to participate when she can.

Utilizing volunteer help effectively requires planning and organization. While parents in the classroom intimidate some teachers, I have found their presence to be supportive and worth the effort it takes to plan their time productively. The students benefit from receiving extra help. Without the consistent assistance the parents provide, it would be difficult to differentiate instruction in the manner I can with parental help. They help students work on make-up work, read a story, work on plays, or play a game to reinforce or build math skills. By their presence, they show students the importance they place on school and education. Parents come out of the experience knowing how material is being presented and take away strategies to help their children at home. They feel welcomed and a part of the educational process.

Parent volunteers directly impact student learning. They can provide immediate attention to a misconception or provide the direct guided practice some students need to understand a concept or skill. They offer support and immediate feedback to keep the student going. Students can get extra practice to secure their understanding of skills. Parents provide regular interaction with small group activities. Without parental involvement in the classroom, I could not accomplish the number of learning activities or projects we are currently doing.

Authors' Party

Each spring, parents, grandparents, and friends gather to celebrate the writing and publishing efforts of our class. The authors' party is a culmination of a year-long project. In my classroom, we have a mini publishing company called The Roadrunner Press and at the end of the year, each student receives a bound anthology of his or her writing. Throughout the year, stories are written, edited, refined, and rewritten. After the stories are shared with classmates, parents who work for our publishing company type up the stories and prepare the anthologies.

At the celebration, each child reads a story of his or her choice using the microphone. We read the stories in the chronological order in which they were written (after practicing in front of our first-grade reading buddies). The stories read at our program give a glimpse into the year we've shared. The audience of relatives and friends offers a warm response. Once the program is over, students eagerly share the rest of their stories with their guests. It is truly a celebration of hard work and effort.

This effort is made possible because of the partnership I have with parents. One of their jobs is to assist students in the editing process and to type up their stories for the anthology. I could not do this project without their assistance. Parents experience firsthand what their children are doing in school, and since our writing encompasses all of the content areas, they quickly get a feel for our whole day. From typing different students' work, they become aware of the diverse views the students take away from the same activity. As the year progresses, more and more of the writing is revised and edited by the students, and the pieces are entered into the book in their handwriting. I continue to use the parents for assistance in revision, editing, and publishing longer texts. They also keep up with binding the stories into the books.

Impact on student learning is evidenced in the quality of writing my students accomplish at the end of the year compared to the writing that begins our anthology. At the beginning of the year, most of the stories are computer generated by parents from the first draft writing of the students. Students recognize the growth they have made as they excitedly share their works with the caring audience that assembles at the authors' party. In the end, students leave second grade knowing they are writers, with a treasured keepsake to prove it.

Family Math Nights

Parents are invited into the school with their child to work on engaging math projects. This provides me with an opportunity to share my philosophy of mathematics with the parents. Most important, families leave with a bank of activities and games that make math learning fun at home.

Math is an area of apprehension and anxiety for many adults. It is a direct correlation to their experience with math instruction. What we know about math learning, problem solving, and communication has changed in the years since the parents of my students were in school. Parents note the change in approach and the difference in the attitude their children have compared to their own attitude to math. They are pleased their children like math and recognize the importance of math in their adult lives. Providing Family Math Night gives parents the ideas and skills they need to supplement, build, and encourage the mathematics skills of their children. Every parent has a math story to tell. I am working to give those stories happier endings.

When students are participating in meaningful and engaging activities, learning is fun and they are more likely to choose to do it. By introducing parents to games and activities, they go away with a bank of ideas to use with their children at home. Whether it is the fraction kit we make, or a quick game of Digit Place, parents leave knowing how to productively assist their child's math learning. They begin to see the importance of mental math, and they take away ideas for implementing math activities in their everyday life.

Parents are more than willing to help their children at home when they know what they can do to help. For the most part, this comfort area has included reading with their child and practicing the infamous spelling words. By providing the Family Math Nights, parents are given ideas on how they can work with their child to improve math skills in fun and engaging ways without the drill of worksheets and flashcards. The activities encourage a diverse sharing of strategies and the license to reason problems from a number of different approaches. Diversity in thinking is encouraged and celebrated. If nothing else, parents leave knowing that it is fine to show students a way to solve problems that may or may not parallel the teacher's explanation. It gives me an opportunity to show them strategies and multiple procedures to problem solutions that are perfectly all right. We are well beyond the "only one right way to a solution" that many of them experienced in school.

In addition to the Family Math Nights, students have the opportunity to borrow the activities and exercises we use in the classroom to take home. I have math bags with drawstrings for the students to carry the take-home games and activities. I can change the games in each bag to match the skills we are working on in the classroom, or as their interests change.

The math bags reinforce the concepts taught in the classroom and allow parents a vehicle to work with their children at home. Feedback has been positive and the demand for take-home activities exceeded my expectations. Additionally, parents get a feel for current trends in mathematics instruction and gain insights into their child's math learning. Parents are part of the learning environment and students get extra practice in an engaging activity.

Billy

Every Family Is a Special Family

Susan Illgen
Grove, Oklahoma

Billy was one of those students you couldn't help but love. Sure, he wore rumpled clothes and his grimy hair fell in untamed locks, but his toothless grin, although the result of tooth decay, was irresistible. It was the first day of kindergarten and love at first sight. Billy's mother followed him through the door, carrying a dirty backpack and only a third of the supplies he needed for kindergarten. She wore sweatpants with holes in them, and as if ashamed, she shied away from conversation with me. Billy's preschool teacher had forewarned me that his family would not be involved in his education because they were poor. "Ah," I thought, "they will be my project this year." Little did I know I would become the project instead.

Billy struggled in school. I spent afternoons tutoring him and sent lengthy homework assignments home, hoping his parents would see the value in assisting Billy with his education. His parents were timid about helping him, they, too, apparently having had trouble in school. When conference time for the first nine weeks came, I just knew they wouldn't show. As a matter of fact, I left the classroom just before their scheduled time to run some errands. However, when I returned to the classroom I found Billy's mom and dad, sitting in our child-sized chairs having clearly showered and dressed in their best clothes. Their efforts quickly told me more than words could ever express. They had a genuine respect for my role as a teacher and were seeking to impress me.

Indeed they did. They seemed slightly embarrassed and awkward, but they listened carefully and asked about helping Billy at home. They confided in me they had their own academic challenges, both of them having gone through the special education programs when they were in school. They clearly felt inadequate and unsure about how to help Billy learn to read. I found myself regretting the assumptions I had made about their involvement and interest in Billy. So, I decided to do something about it. My natural inclination was to find a way to get them involved with our school that would validate what they could do and make them feel important to our classroom. Intuitively, I knew I needed their support because most likely Billy would be placed in special education classes. Gaining their trust would be essential.

We had begun a unit on community helpers, so I asked Billy's dad, a truck driver, if he would bring his semi to school for the students to see. I also invited him to share why it was important for him as a truck driver to read and write and to share ways math was relevant to his work. Billy's dad, at first, was hesitant, but the more we talked, the more excited he became. His eyes began to sparkle, his speech quickened, and by the time they left he was making grand plans for our classroom adventure with his semi.

On the day of his presentation, the students and I walked to the bus barn, Billy bounding ahead of the class. We were greeted by his freshly shaven dad, dressed in his best clothes and bubbling with excitement. The students explored the cab of his truck, checked out the various instruments and compartments, and occasionally blared the truck horn. Then, he gathered the students in a group and shared how important it was to get a "good education." He showed them his travel log, expense reports, and paperwork required for his job. He and his wife had painstakingly made travel logs for each of the students (something he did by instinct, not knowing what a powerful tool it was). He shared that he had to know how to work with money and mileage and how to calculate and add. The students embraced him when it was time to go as if he were their best friend. He honked his truck horn as he drove off, I'm sure feeling prouder and more confident than ever before.

Of all the community helpers that have visited my classroom, my students' all time favorite was the visit from the truck driver. For me, it was the first time I realized the power I had as a teacher leader in affecting parents and the community. I, as well, left that day prouder and more confident than ever before. I was a *professional.* I had the expertise to educate and the power to motivate not only my students but also my community. Billy and his family approached learning differently after the truck visit. Throughout the year, Billy's mother and father regularly visited the classroom, reading to students, handling classroom pets, and helping in learning centers. Billy, as well, had a renewed sense of confidence, evident in his efforts in the classroom and the newfound respect he had gained from his peers.

Poverty and school failure are closely linked. The challenge to involve parents in education is formidable, but to involve parents of lower socioeconomic status is an even greater challenge. Realizing the greatest resource I have as an educator is not in the curriculum I teach, or in the knowledge I hold, but in my students' families and community has transformed the attitude I carry towards their involvement in education. It simply is not an option. I learned as a leader in education I must step forward, put aside my assumptions about my students and their families, and purpose to engage them meaningfully in education. By validating the time and talents of our classroom families, I provide the opportunity to educate the community about what is really going on in the classroom. When the community sees learning is fun and exciting, they can't help but support education, my teaching, and student learning in every way possible.

The key to effecting change in education is to provide a real picture of today's classrooms, its students, and ultimately its needs. All too often, as leaders in education, we have taken the wrong approach. Our whining has created barriers of defense and indifference. However, meaningful community and family involvement can break down those barriers. Change begins when we assert a genuine interest in and understanding of our students' cultural backgrounds and implement it through clear and respectful communication, emphasizing teamwork and sensitivity to families' needs. Service opportunities for both families and the community should be long term. This allows for relationship building and the opportunity to convey interest and respect for the concerns of family and community volunteers. The result is the community and school working together to meet the needs of our children. I have endorsed reciprocal involvement with family and community in many ways. Listed below are a few ways to get started.

Family Involvement

1.   Create many opportunities for families to gain information about what is actually happening in the classroom: class videos to check out, family nights to learn about how you teach specific subject areas, newsletters with a clip-off section for family comments, open house before PTA meetings, family volunteers in the classroom and on field trips, class-made books to check out with a comment section in the front, family guest readers who are on lunch break (doesn't interfere with their work schedule), "special day" centers coordinated by families (e.g., sewing center, Olympics center, baking center), or "Families as Teachers" day.

2.   Create many opportunities to have positive two-way communication with your families at home or beyond school hours: call them to tell them something positive about their student, utilize family interviews and surveys as a means to get to know them better, use a spiral-bound notebook to facilitate two-way communication between you and your students' families (students should keep it in their backpack, number the pages, and be sure to copy any "important pages" for your records . . . they occasionally disappear), use e-mail or create a class Web page, allow your students to communicate with their families through e-mail at school, host family cook-outs, plan special family field trips on weekends and evenings that highlight unique cultural experiences (no busses needed!), provide "at- home" projects for families who wish to assist in the classroom but work during the day, print business cards with your contact information so parents know how to contact you, or incorporate home visits as a form of conferencing.

Community Involvement

1.   Create many opportunities for the community to gain information about what is actually going on in the classroom: avoid whining (be positive about education and what you are doing as a teacher); invite

guest speakers (such as business professionals) to use their lunch break for reading to the class or sharing their occupation; be quick to tell your class's success stories in public (while remembering confidentiality rules); invite your school board, local business owners, and community service organizations to all of your open houses; have students contact local businesses by writing letters and asking questions about their work (interviewing); or contact the press personally about the exciting ways your students are learning (be sure to offer pictures and thank them anytime they publicize your classroom happenings).

2. Create many opportunities for your students to give back to the community: make routine visits to the senior citizen center or nursing home, clean up a neighborhood park in conjunction with a group such as the Rotary Club or Kiwanis, collect canned goods for your local food bank (have students take the canned food themselves and help with stocking shelves), make class books for younger learners and have students read to them, host a disability awareness day for students to gain information about people who live with disabilities and to become more sympathetic to their issues, have students write thank you notes to heroic community helpers, or collect pet supplies for a local animal shelter.

Helpful Tips

- Ensure that every interaction with the community and your students' families takes a positive spin.
- Understand the cultural background and unique challenges of your volunteers.
- Work towards engaging long-term commitment.
- Reciprocate, Reciprocate, Reciprocate! (Have students volunteer for community projects.)
- Practice your speaking skills. Effective communication is the key to healthy relationships.
- Practice inquiring of the community and parents their concerns.
- Ensure families have easy access to information about their children's classroom obligations and responsibilities.

CHAPTER 3

Encouraging Hands-On Learning in Science and Technology

 Students and Research

Using Students to Create a Science Research Program

Michael Corcoran
Jersey City, New Jersey

The best practice method that I know has evolved gradually over the past decade. Today the Science Research Program at Dickinson High School is recognized at the local, state, and national levels for excellence in science. In 2003, two of the students in this program were the national team winners ($100,000) in the Siemens-Westinghouse Science and Technology Competition. One of the students attends Harvard University on a full scholarship. In 2004, our research group won more than half of all the medals awarded at the Regional (ISEF) Science Fair and the Best Overall of the Fair award. This excellence has been attained through a gradual and meticulous process that is based firmly in the scientific method, one that specifies a question and outlines the sequence of steps needed to answer it. By adhering to conventions of objective observation, control of extraneous variance, and unbiased analysis of data, the scientific method ensures reproducibility of findings via empirical evidence.

It should be noted that decisions must be made as one proceeds; hence, adherence to all steps is not mandatory, nor in many situations prudent. Researchers must make decisions as they proceed. Nevertheless, by using the broad canvas of the scientific method, my students gain insight into the way science operates and by following the sequential steps can grasp how casual observations lead to hypotheses, data gathering, and ultimate support for or refutation of explanations of events in the world around them. This enables them to "see" how their "simple" high school research project may lead one day to their findings being accepted into the body of scientific knowledge. Actually, I have employed this conceptual framework throughout the development and implementation of my program to make decisions and to address problems more directly and efficiently. It hasn't been easy going, but it models the process of "doing" science, which often spends years probing a single issue before satisfactory results are obtained.

My Science Research Program is part of a Science Magnet of approximately 150 students at a large urban high school of over 3,000 students. The program offers five research classes and a variety of methods to screen and select students who express a career interest in science. All entering students must take an Introduction to Research class, which focuses on the fundamentals of scientific inquiry. Upon completion of this class, students are divided into two groups based on a combination of achievement and a desire to "do" independent science research. Those selected to continue enter the Science Fair Level for the next three years. Those not elected to continue at this level take a second year of science research and produce a research project for an in-house science fair. After the second year, unless they rediscover an interest in science research, their contact with the program ends. The Science Fair students form the heart of our program and I will describe how we developed our current program.

In 1993, a decision was made to start a research program for our Science Magnet students to increase participation and improve performance at our local county science fair. We certainly had students of proven academic excellence with a professed interest in science. And although we had some students who entered the fair each year, there was scant interest within the Magnet program for student research and modest success at the fair. It was my aim to create a program for science research that would equal the work done in universities and research laboratories. To accomplish this goal, I set up a series of student-led committees to discuss and clearly articulate our objectives and evaluate whether we had the necessary resources, desire, and drive to establish a program whose main purpose would be to foster and produce original and ambitious science research projects. I found a great deal of interest in my first class of students to initiate and continue the process over the succeeding years. The program did grow and mature, primarily through students who were willing to continuously evaluate, discover the necessary information to create and propel change, and then to put it into practice in their own work. Let me outline this process as it exists for this academic cycle.

In the spring, after the annual science fair, students select a topic for the following year's research project. Throughout the year students scan periodicals, Web sites, and The New York Times Science Times weekly to identify project ideas. Over the course of a year we end up with hundreds of possibilities; we read them and decide whether they would work for a student research project. After this screening process, they are subdivided according to the fourteen INTEL ISEF categories and placed in folders. This effectively eliminates the enormous amount of time that is usually spent searching for a project idea and simultaneously ensures that projects have originality, complexity, and interest to the student and public as well. When a student selects a project idea from these folders, the next step is to perform a critical evaluation of its practicality and potential. This procedure enables the students to fully explore their interest in the topic and to make an informed decision about work that will become a year-long commitment. They write a proposal and devise two experimental approaches for its completion; assess all materials, cost, and availability; and do a limited review of pertinent literature. After this process, a decision is made by the class to approve or reject the project. If the project is accepted, the class discusses and decides on an agenda to be followed and the next steps the student should take.

The summer is devoted to a thorough search of pertinent literature that is deeply rooted in the debate surrounding the research topic. I teach my students a method for reading research literature that helps them develop confidence and understanding. I have adapted a strategy from an article in *The Journal of Chemical Education* (February, 1997) by Bruce G. Drake. This article outlines a framework, known as KENSHU, for reading complex and obtuse scientific literature. The KENSHU method provides step-by-step prompts that guide the student to search for relevant points. The basic steps are (1) take a recent scientific article and divide it into sections, (2) read and discuss a single section with a more experienced classmate, (3) identify and define unknown words, (4) continue step 3 until all sections are finished, (5) prepare a one-page summary of the article with key graphs and tables, and (6) present the "findings" of the article to the class. They are expected to employ KENSHU for all their literature search summaries. In the fall, an oral defense of their literature is required. Here each student describes the debate in a mini-conference, provides written (KENSHU) summaries, and justifies the relevance of the literature to his or her project.

The next areas to consider are the experimental approach, data form, and data analysis. Students identify the type of inquiry: descriptive, correlational, or experimental, and in some cases a combination of them. Prior to conducting their main experimental study, they must choose their hypotheses, experimental approach, and data analysis at two levels, descriptive and inferential, and identify the specific inferential test they will employ to establish significance for their data. We use the Internet to obtain theoretical information about the most reliable test for their data and use spreadsheets to perform and analyze them. Here, again, we establish "masters" of every possible inferential statistical test by requiring the senior students to familiarize themselves with a single test and how to perform and interpret it. Subsequently, they act as "experts" for a specific inferential test and are able to assist and guide their underclassmates through this often difficult and daunting process. Now performing the main study is a predefined task.

The final area that requires collaborative input is the preparation of the research project for competition. We have developed a video archive of student presentations and select several effective (and some not-so-effective) presentations for students to view, dissect, critique, and discuss. Students are welcome to borrow videos of presentations to prepare their own. Upper-level students present to beginners who provide a written evaluation, which helps them to develop and refine critical thinking skills vital for their own success. We pretend that each project is the only one our school will be entering in the fair and thus must represent our entire program. The discussion that follows primarily aims to identify ways to improve both the presentation and the project board. Students are encouraged to model their presentations on effective and successful models from the past. In the final days before the fair, students are required to present in varied situations (English class, AP Chemistry, etc.) in order to reach out beyond their science research peers. We host an in-house practice fair at which students present to almost everyone in the school. In addition, some students present online to an expert mentor.

For my students in the Science Research Program, it is a perpetual struggle to maintain our eminence in science. Thus, each year after the fair we discuss our limitations based upon both our successes and failures. We identify the reasons for *either* outcome and create a list of problem areas that we will focus on for the "new" year of science competition.

Our Program Objectives

- To challenge students to a very high academic level.
- To develop problem-solving and critical thinking skills.
- To encourage and train students to conduct individual scientific investigation of their own design.
- To develop the ability to use investigative techniques in any field in science.

- To learn that accuracy and statistical analysis of evidence is critical to their solution and its defense.
- To establish collaborative links with colleges, universities, and the private sector.
- To offer students an opportunity to present their work in a variety of competitive situations with poise and sophistication.
- To create an award-winning project that reflects originality and adds knowledge to the subject under study.

CELLLSS (Creating Experiences in Life, Learning, and Laboratory Science Skills) for Girls

Turning Middle and High School Girls On to Science

Michal Robinson
Birmingham, Alabama

While researching the gender gap in science and technology, I found that female students lose interest in these disciplines at the middle school level. In an effort to encourage girls to pursue science and technology in secondary school, I decided to use high school girls to engage girls at the middle school level. Girls were chosen from tenth-grade biology classes to be facilitators and role models to younger girls. They continued this volunteer work through their senior year. With a teacher fellowship from the American Association of University Women, CELLLSS was created.

The goals are

- To develop an innovative setting in the form of a summer support program that will offer opportunities primarily for girls to pursue science and technology interest while enhancing personal growth (self-confidence and self-efficacy).
- To implement a gender equitable outreach program in science and technology, primarily for Huffman High School's feeder schools, that is cohesive with its high school program.

Huffman High School science students were trained to develop science and technology enrichment activities that fulfill the Alabama

Course of Study objectives to be implemented in a summer science and technology program at the high school, at the feeder middle schools, and in community-based programs.

Summer Program

In the spring, the girls and I outline a curriculum for two one-week summer programs in science and technology. The first week is for girls only; boys are included in the second week. At scheduled outreach activities with eighth-grade students at the feeder middle schools, we encourage students to attend the summer program.

Once the summer program begins, high school girls arrive early each day to set up activities and to greet students. Using inquiry-based learning, students are introduced to basic laboratory skills. For example, students are given four brands of toilet paper, a rubber band, a small cup, and some pennies. They are then asked to use the scientific method to determine which brand of toilet paper is strongest when wet. Because the girls are not being pressured to receive a grade but are simply free to learn, they are much more creative with their work. Each student keeps a reflective journal of the day's activities. Another basic skill learned during the summer program is metric measurement. Each pair of students is given a Dino polymer that absorbs water. On Day 1, they measure length, width, height, area, volume (using over-flow), mass, and density of their Dino and then place it in a storage bag of water. As soon as they arrive each morning, students take measurements to see how much their Dino has grown and record information in a data table. At the end of the week, graphs are constructed and analyses are made. Wonderful opportunities for using metric measurements for length, volume, and mass are used. Students gain practice using a balance, a graduated cylinder, and other laboratory equipment as well.

In the *girls only* group, girls get to do more than just be recorders of data. One of our local universities loaned DNA electrophoresis equipment and micropipettes so that incoming ninth-grade students actually get a chance to understand DNA technology firsthand by performing simple electrophoresis experiments. This past summer, another college sent over one of its professors to train our participants in the use of Geographic Information System (GIS) technology. They manipulated software to compare climate data in several geographic regions. Needless to say, it was one of their favorite learning experiences.

A plus is that the students invited to participate in our free program are students we expect to attend our school in the fall. The high school students answer questions that the new students may have about high school, offer advice on how to succeed in high school, and take them on a tour of the school. The participants feel that they have an edge because they have already learned their way around campus. After the program participants leave, the high school volunteers clean up the laboratory and prepare for the next day. We discuss the day's activities and decide whether we need to make changes in any of the next day's lessons. The girls are totally involved in the decision making and are well-prepared for each day's activities.

We have run this program for two years. The middle school girls enjoy a positive support setting that encourages them to pursue science and technology interests with peers who have the same desires. They also respond extremely well to being taught by high school students.

Community Programs

During the school year, several tenth- and eleventh-grade girls and boys volunteer to participate in the science and technology outreach program for younger children. It involves staying after school twice a week to plan, learn, and practice hands-on science experiments for community programs such as YMCA afterschool care, Girl Scouts, YMCA Middle School Academy, and Delta Academy. One such program was Eco-Discovery, a Saturday ecology-based program at a not-so-nearby Girl Scout camp. The students and I designed Eco-Discovery to meet many of the requirements for the Girl Scout's Watershed and Waterdrop badges. Because they had to actually take a group of girls and teach a concept, planning this program required studying the science so that they could answer participants' questions. One investigation required them to explore how layers of earth act as a filter for groundwater. The high school students showed them how to make models of the Earth's filtration system and then test them with various substances. Another investigation required them to use water quality kits to test for nitrates, phosphates, and dissolved oxygen in water. The high school students also made a PowerPoint presentation of water facts.

For Women's History Month, we highlighted Rosalind Franklin (X-ray diffraction of DNA) and performed experiments spooling DNA from foods. We make what we call a "DNA smoothie" from bananas that students use to spool DNA (from a workshop attended at a National Science Teachers Association conference). While they are going through the steps in the experiment, we provide refreshing smoothies for them to drink. It is exciting to see them discover that DNA is actually in food and that they have been eating it. Parents who stay for our activities also get involved.

Our Halloween Chemystery (a Flinn Scientific activity) is the most fun. The high school students and I dress in Halloween costumes when we present these experiments. We explain the mystery of some Halloween tricks with chemistry. We always end this program by making slime or superballs.

CELLLSS is a win-win situation for all involved. The younger children are inspired by seeing high school students actually *doing and understanding* science. They identify with someone closer to their age and respond positively to learning. In our *girls only* groups, the self-confidence to jump in and perform hands-on activities increases. By the end of a program with us, students who come in afraid that they would make a mistake, do something wrong, or that someone will make fun of them leave the program more self-confident and self-assured. Another important aspect of our program is that girls (and boys) are introduced to female scientists as well as male scientists so that stereo-types about scientists and gender are discarded. We receive positive evaluations of the program. The girls who attend the summer program always state that they did not want to attend; they were there because their parents made them come. Upon attending, they learn science in a fun and interesting format and, most important to their family, they became familiar with their new school. Most of them expressed an interest in working with the CELLLSS program in high school.

High school students benefit as well. They gain greater insight into science concepts by actually teaching them. In addition to science skills, they learn responsibility, maturity, and self-confidence. They stay after school to work on experiments just out of the joy of accom-plishment. Participants do not receive grades for their work. Because my first group graduates this year, I have no data on how this affects their postsecondary education; however, I do hope that some will pursue a science or technology major. Most important for them, however, is how this program transforms them. For example, one of the first girls chosen to work with CELLLSS had great potential but did mediocre work in her tenth-grade classes. She was shy about public speaking and had limited laboratory skills. In addition, she had been known to cut classes constantly and had lost credits due to lack of attendance. Since working with CELLLSS, she has made a complete turnaround in behavior and attitude. She is completely confident in a lab setting. In fact, she is the lab manager of our program and trains the new volunteers as we get them. What is most remarkable is this story: Last year, she was enrolled in the required speech class and had to make the usual speech to the class about some topic. At the end of class, she immediately came to my room to tell me that since working with me, she is no longer nervous about public speaking. It was only when she had to give her speech that she realized that being a part of CELLLSS had advantages for her as well. As she gave to others, she also received.

Helpful Tips

- Seek seed money to assist with equipment and supplies.
- Plan ahead.
- Obtain parent permission for volunteers.
- When presenting an outreach program at a different site, meet with the person in charge to adequately plan activities. Visit sites ahead of time, if possible. Make sure that outlets, water, and safety equipment are available. Bring your own, if needed.
- When planning a summer program, obtain emergency and medical information from participants and volunteers.
- Prepare a curriculum with specific outcomes in mind.
- Always provide participants with an evaluation.

For resources and information on Gender Gaps and Education, see AAUW Educational Foundation, American Association of University Women, www.aauw.org.

🐚 Voyaging Through Curriculum

Michelle Evans
Huntsville, Utah

Achieving National Board Certification brings with it a greater understanding of the importance of analyzing and reflecting on what we do. Working to consciously consider what I was doing helped me become a better teacher. I knew it could have the same effect on my students. This was not a case of, "Kids, I had to, so you have to!" It was a case of, "Good news! I am a better teacher for having gone through the process of National Board Certification. Now you get to benefit from what I learned. You can become better learners yourselves!" Great. Inspirational! But how do you convince 31 twelve-year-olds of that? How do you motivate 120 sixth graders from the whole school to get excited about reflecting and analyzing? My teammates and I were about to find out.

The new school year promised to be exciting and challenging for several reasons. First, our whole approach to teaching was going to change. We would be teaching through a new "vehicle," literally—we taught using space ships that we built inside our classrooms. Second, I was teaching information technology this year to half the sixth grade. Third, I was teaching science for the first time in many years, again to half the sixth grade. State core science objectives changed radically for the new school year, too. Everything seemed fresh. I was feeling especially green with inexperience despite my 17 years of teaching. The only way to handle it was to learn with the kids. I wanted to include student reflecting and analyzing in as many ways as possible because I knew how beneficial it would be.

Let me explain the space ships first. My sixth-grade teammate and I had spent the previous summer building space ships in sections of our classrooms. Why? I had visited an elaborate Space Camp in another district and it was phenomenal. This camp looked like a set from Star Trek. It had been built as a result of individual ideas, community effort, and funding from the Christa McAuliffe Foundation. Our rural school was too far away to be able to afford to go to places like that very often. The cost of busing alone would be astronomical. The camp curriculum repeated daily, so one visit was enough for the year. But I wanted our kids to have that experience, so I wrote a grant application and the students worked on some class fundraisers. We invited parents and took the whole sixth grade. Parent enthusiasm was high when they and their kids saw the camp and caught the vision of what we wanted to do. When we returned home, our sixth graders earned more money through some school activities. I had a little grant money left over, and we began to reach into the community for help.

Our thinking was, "Why not try to build something at our school that could be a part of everyday classes? If we had two small ships right in our own school, sixth graders could 'voyage' through curriculum whenever we wanted. We could use different disciplines as themes for each voyage, sometimes science, sometimes math, sometimes reading, or whatever!" By writing grant applications and receiving some awards, my teaching partner and I already had 10 computers in each of our rooms. In order to build the ships, we placed the computers on a raised, 10 feet by 15 feet rectangular platform that houses five computers on a side. Two walls of the ships are our classroom walls where two corners meet. A third wall is a half wall four feet high with a net curtain dropped from the ceiling to make it seem enclosed. The fourth wall is an entryway with two steps up to a darkroom door. A darkroom door is tubular in shape and twists shut so that when a person steps inside, the door closes shut from behind as it opens in front. Inner walls are painted an eerie blue, lighted by blue theater track lights around the ceiling and decorated with papier-mâché planets suspended from the ceiling. All computers have space scene wallpaper and screen savers to add to the ambience.

The PTA sewed costume smocks for different jobs on the ship like captain, engineers, crewmembers, ambassadors, and, of course, aliens. We hammered, cut, sawed, and drilled our way to the coming of the next school year. Three Eagle Scout awards, 20 business partnerships, a few grants, a score of space costumes, and two space-age looking 10-seat computer ships later, we were ready for action. We wanted to teach in a way that many subject areas would become virtual experience lessons. We taught language arts in the ships that year. We integrated another subject area as we tackled science this year.

We decided to create projects wherein the students would go on educational missions. They would fly through time in order to be there at important moments in history. These moments might include spending time with Copernicus, Galileo, Alexander Fleming, Louis Pasteur, John Glenn, and even Laika the first space dog. We solicited parents, community members, and other students to study these and other main characters and then appear for the space adventures. The scientist would appear in costume, answer questions, lead an experiment or two, and then pose for pictures with the "crew." Students would research other aspects of the findings of these scientists and do some experiments of their own. Each student kept a journal. When space ship time was over, they would go back to their seats and write about what they had experienced. This would allow another group to go into the ship to start on their educational adventures.

Students grouped to read journal entries. They discussed and then compiled the information into booklets about sixth-grade core objectives as they had experienced them in the ship, with a scientist, and experimenting outside and inside the ship. This reflection and analysis became the real learning. Students learned from each others' points of view, corrected misconceptions, demonstrated organizational skills, and worked to put it all together in a pleasing format. Students used a digital camera to take pictures of what they worked on and inserted those pictures into the booklet. At first, my colleagues and I set up the activities and step-by-step guides to what happened in the ships. The space ships were used to research, inquire, and write. But eventually students begged to be given a concept and then allowed to act out their own experiences dealing with the objective being investigated. Students wrote facts, reflected and analyzed their thinking, and concluded with how these scientific events have benefited their lives. We went from "Why do we care about Galileo and all those old dudes?" to "I wonder if I can change the world like Louis Pasteur?"

An entire class period discussion occurred when a famous English astronomer from the 1700s named James Bradley appeared one day. Bradley had drawn the night sky every night for a year. In doing so he noticed the positions of the stars and how the positions repeated yearly. One student queried, "Has anyone ever really thought about something for that long a time and then done something for a whole year like that?" As a team we relished every moment of science! We laughed. We messed up. But mostly we ran as fast as we could to keep up with the momentum of what we had launched.

Year-end district core test results were the highest in our district. Every special needs student in our classes passed science. Indeed, each one eagerly participated in every aspect of science. Students wrote and participated who had not written or even lifted a finger to work in any other subject in any past year. Behavior problems were minimized. Gifted students excelled as they became masters of their own learning. Parents thoroughly delighted in and commented on what they learned as they read the booklets. Student journals replete with reflection and analysis went home as treasured portfolio items from an incredible year. We placed copies of the books in our media center and on our Web site for one year for future generations to enjoy. The booklets created evidence of wonderful learning experiences, memories, and the synergy that is naturally achieved when learning is maximized. (Access http://VES6thGrade.net and look for "Science Quest" under "Projects.") Unfortunately, though, only some items are left for display as we used server space for more projects. More projects? Isn't teaching great?

Helpful Tips

- Be teachable.
- Be excited about what you are doing.
- Be a team player!

▧ Teaming Up for Success

Karen Neely
Pearl, Mississippi

Education has arrived at a time of accountability, making sure that each child achieves to the maximum of his or her ability. The halls of schools are echoing "no child left behind." As science department chairperson, I made the decision that none of the biology teachers in my department would get left behind when preparing our biology students for the mandated state biology test that is given each April. I have developed techniques that motivate students, hold their attention, and cause them to place scientific concepts into long-term memory. I have shared these techniques not only with my department but with our junior high teachers and other teachers across the state. Pearl High School state biology scores have been in the top 10 of the 154 school districts for the past 10 years.

The biology teachers at PHS had four major concerns about preparing their students for the biology subject area test. The first concern was that the curriculum from the junior high did not line up with the high school curriculum for biology. The second concern was that their students were not organized learners. The third concern was that they could not keep their students' attention. The fourth concern was that they could not get their students to study at home. As the department chairperson, I felt that it was my job to address these concerns and help make the biology teachers' job less stressful and more enjoyable.

Because there was a lack of communication between the teachers at the two schools, the junior high teachers did not know what part of the eighth-grade curriculum the biology teachers needed emphasized. To remedy this situation and with support from the administration at both schools, I invited the junior high teachers to attend a workshop held at the high school, in which the two groups of teachers teamed up to identify overlapping concepts between the curricula. After identifying these concepts, a biology teacher was paired with a junior high teacher and given the task of developing a lesson plan for that concept. Using the Internet as a resource, the teachers enjoyed working as a team to solve a problem that had existed for many years.

When the workshop was over, and much to the delight of all involved, a lesson plan resource notebook had been developed that would be used to teach the biology concepts to the eighth-grade students. Participants decided that the eighth-grade students would keep these completed lessons in a notebook that would be passed up to the high school each year. The first May following the workshop, the high school received over 200 notebooks filled with documentation of the concepts that were taught in the eighth grade. Having their notebooks follow them to high school has made the eighth graders aware that there is an important connection between their eighth-grade and freshman years. Because the two groups of teachers were able to work together to bridge a gap in the curriculum, our freshman students are now much more successful in biology. From this experience with our junior high, I have developed a workshop called Bridging the Curriculum Gap Between Middle School and High School, which I have enjoyed presenting across the state.

Our next challenge was to deal with students' organizational skills, which are necessary for meaningful learning to occur. To encourage the students to become more organized, I developed a science notebook that all the science teachers now require their students to keep throughout the school year. In this notebook, students keep class notes, activity sheets, returned assessments, and other materials in an organized manner. All of the science teachers follow the same basic guidelines so the students become accustomed to the organizational skills required to keep the notebook. Students receive a major grade for the notebook every nine weeks. The notebook, which is called a major concept notebook for that subject, is truly a portfolio of the student's work throughout the year. Students, teachers, and parents are very proud of these notebooks at the end of each year.

As all educators know, keeping students' attention becomes more difficult each year. Today, students are accustomed to media entertainment, which is tough competition for educators. I encouraged the biology teachers to try several techniques to help students stay involved in their lessons. One technique is to announce an "attention test" in the middle of a lecture. Students are not warned when the test will be given. I ask them 11 questions (not really in depth). They can miss one and still make 100%. This technique has worked well. Initially, the students did not like the idea, but they soon realized that the tests were easy when they were paying attention.

Another technique that I developed is called "hot seat." When we finish a major concept, I pass out vocabulary cards to the students. When I say the definition, the student with that word has to come to the front of the room and display the word for the rest of the class to see. They all look and listen and when we finish, I pass them out again. The repetition helps the students store the vocabulary in their long-term memory.

A final activity I use to get students up and moving is a technique I developed called "wall learning." I use this activity when the students have facts that can be sorted. For example, when we are studying mitosis, the students are given a typed sheet of characteristics of the various stages—but the characteristics have been scrambled on the page. The students work in pairs to cut out and sort the characteristics of the four stages. The characteristics are then taped under the correct stage on the wall. After checking their work, I have the students independently sort the characteristics.

Probably the hardest job I face is motivating students to study. To help with this problem, I developed the idea of "lines for success." After tests are returned to students, I ask them to write the questions and corrected answers 20 times each. After explaining the reasons behind the lines to their parents and to the administration, I find that this idea really works. The majority of students have decided that it is easier to study for a test than to write the lines for success. When the lines are completed, the students receive a homework grade of 100. Grades in the science department have improved since we started this technique.

Developing new concepts and methods for a school to use is only part of the process. One must remember that teachers in a department are individuals, and they must be inspired to want to make changes and to work as a team. Thought must be given to the leadership style and methods to be used with the staff before implementing new teaching techniques. My success as a department chairperson would not have been possible if the teachers I work with were not willing to be team players. By using these different approaches to learning, the Pearl High School teachers have not only become one of the top biology departments in our state, but have become a team of educators who have one common goal as well. That goal is success for all our students.

Helpful Tips

- Get the curriculum for the middle school and meet with the teachers to brainstorm how they can help you. Talk to both your principal and the middle school principal about the importance of curriculum alignment.
- Communicate with the parents to let them know any new technique that you are going to use in your classroom, and explain to them why you are using it.

- Use plastic notebooks and not folders for the concept note-books. Give the students a list of rules to follow. Grade the notebooks once every nine weeks. Use a rubric that you have also given to the students.
- Laminate "hot seat" and "wall learning" activities. You will only have to make them once.
- Explain to the students that you will not accept poorly writ-ten "lines for success" and that they will have to rewrite any that are not legible.

Growing Community Ties Through Gardening

Kristy Kidd
Little Rock, Arkansas

As a teacher, I never thought to connect my community and my school with a garden. To be a part of such an exciting project sort of fell into my lap, and it has turned out to be one of the most positive experiences of my teaching career. The Dunbar Community Garden was established to give people in an urban neighborhood an opportu-nity to have their own plot of land in order to grow produce. One of the founders of the project, Pratt Remmel, had the idea to include the local schools by having the students work in the garden and learn a hands-on lesson at the same time. Since outdoor teaching has always been a part of my curriculum, I jumped at the chance to be a part of the program. Over the years, the Dunbar Community Garden Project has turned into a valuable asset for tying the community with my school while encouraging parents to become involved in their child-ren's activities and interests.

Once a month my students go to the garden for a lesson during their science class. After each lesson on topics such as worm compost-ing, caring for chickens, or harvesting wheat, the students complete sev-eral tasks around the garden. I am always amazed at how little exposure middle school students have had to any sort of gardening activity. For many of them, it is the first time that they have handled or planted seedlings, harvested produce, or even dug in the soil. Once the various tasks are completed, the class gets to sample a food that was grown, harvested, and cooked in the garden. We have eaten cooked mustard greens, tossed salad, pesto sauce, gumbo, and flatbread. The best part of the experience is that everything, or almost everything, in the snack was grown, harvested, and assembled or cooked by the students. Because of their involvement in the entire process, the students are willing to try a wider variety of foods than their parents ever imagined. The first year that I introduced the Dunbar Garden Program to my middle school, I had parents calling me to ask what I did to entice their children to try vegetables. It seems that many students went home after eating salad in the garden and asked their parents if they could start making the salad at home.

A natural connection with the community was made as surpluses of crops were grown in the plots set aside for the schools. Students began taking the extra produce to the nearby community center to share with the elderly people who came to play checkers or attend classes there during the day. The students also took produce home to share with their families. As the garden grew to include chickens and worms, the students were able to sell the eggs and worm compost as well as produce at the River Market downtown. The money earned by the children was used for garden maintenance and upkeep.

Parents soon began to drop by to see what the Dunbar Garden was all about because their children could not stop talking about their adventures. The number of students and parents that volunteered to help in the garden after school steadily increased. Neighborhood children had a safe and productive place to spend time after school with adults who could serve as mentors.

The number of classes from my middle school participating at the Dunbar Garden has increased from one to ten. That means that around 250 students are exposed to outdoor education and making community ties each month. I feel extremely lucky to be a part of this program, and I have no doubt that it will continue to be a positive influence on many people.

Helpful Tips

- See what programs are already in existence that interest you. There is no need to start from scratch if your class can become connected with a program that someone else has started.
- Start small and use your students as communicators. If they are interested in what is going on, they will spread the word and participation will grow.
- Try to put the children in charge as much as possible. When students see the connection between a completed task and positive results, they take ownership and are encouraged to continue.

Online Collaboration Benefits Students and Teachers

Classrooms Across the World

Janet Barnstable
Oak Park, Illinois

"I don't have time for extras; my students have to do well on the tests!" Sound familiar? It may even have been something you've said, or at least thought. How in the world do you fit an online collaboration, with a teaching partner you've never met, into your busy schedule? It is more work, and it does take time, but everyone involved is engaged in authentic learning that can be shared with the world. Not surprisingly, students value this relevant learning and strive to do better. Can I say empirically that their test results improve? Probably not, but I can say that their love of learning improves, as does their willingness to search for answers.

Participating in online collaborations can motivate students far better than any textbook, parent, or teacher. Students are teachers as well as learners. One major role for the teacher is to help students accept the responsibility for teaching and learning English. The English as a Second Language (ESL) student benefits from communicating with real English speakers, and native speakers work harder than they ever did before, asking other students to check their grammar and word usage and using spell check. They read the material they are posting a second time to be sure that they haven't made a foolish mistake. As Andrew (13) said, "Many of our foreign friends are still learning English, and by not talking slang we are helping them understand the language." This was further clarified by Megan (12) who added, "We need to use proper English or they might get confused because they might not get what we mean." This doesn't happen automatically, but students are proud to become models of correctness. It helps to practice first with classmates. Starting small makes holding on to your commitment doable.

Once communication has begun, many areas of the curriculum are woven naturally into the collaboration. If you are studying biomes, tell your partners about where you live and ask them about their environment. It's likely that they are in a different biome. The students in Israel will be able to tell you as much about their region as any textbook, and it's coming from a friend talking with a friend. Map skills increase when students want to know where Novosibirsk, Russia is located. They will cross 12 time zones and two continents to find it. There is an increased appreciation of cultural and political differences as students discuss elections, holidays, or length of the school day. Do students in Japan really have more school?

Ever had a tough time getting students to learn metric conversions? How about having them share recipes with their global partners? Almost anywhere else in the world our measurements need conversion to the metric equivalents so that partners will be able to cook correctly. How far is it to school? Well, are we talking miles? Kilometers? Feet?

You get the idea. Anything that has to be taught has more meaning if it has relevance and immediacy of use to the students who are learning. Learning to put information into a spreadsheet and making a graph just does not compare with collecting data about smoking by teens and creating a chart that shows the effectiveness of programs designed to keep cigarettes out of the hands of students.

It is great when partners send pictures, and if the students create a Web site on a topic of mutual interest, they find out about copyright laws and how to write for permission to use someone else's images. (These are important business letter writing skills.)

Kids aren't the only ones to benefit; teachers, too, will find that they are inspired by their partners to do things that they never thought of before. Sharing the teaching is really enjoyable and you're no longer alone, even though your teacher partner might be working while you're asleep. Actually, the greatest teacher benefit is to see the student learning through the project interactions.

Is it more work? Yes, you do have to spend time talking with your partner teacher so that you share learning goals for your students. That does not mean that both groups of students have the same goals. An ESL class in Kiev might have as a goal to learn to use English correctly, while a class in Illinois might be studying the breakup of the Soviet Union. Whatever the goals, you do have to take time to set them and to see how they fit into the prescribed curriculum. On the other hand, you'll see much more parental interest; involved students will talk with their parents about the projects.

How Do You Find Partners?

Here are some of the best:

- www.gsn.org. "Clearinghouse for content, partners, tools, and effective implementation strategies to support online shared learning."
- www.globaldreamers.org. Simple collaborations, bulletin board, storyblog, picture galleries.
- www.friendsandflags.org. Structured groups of two to five classes formed with specific collaboration topics to complete.
- www.epals.org. Global network "connecting 191 countries in classroom-to-classroom projects and cross-cultural learning."
- www.gigglepotz.com/cc.htm. Class Connect; teacher registers class and selects a class match.

Our Ongoing Projects

Participants accepted at any time:

- CyberTeen (www.op97.org/cyberteen): an online cultural sharing magazine by and for teens and their teachers.
- CyberDictionary (www.op97.org/instruct/ftcyber): fairy, folk, and other tales illustrated by primary students.

Helpful Tips

- Agree on short "Netiquette" rules that include such things as "use school English."
- Understand ESL students will make mistakes and, above all, be understanding.
- Choose topics so that everyone can learn.
- Have students working on more than one project at a time. Online collaborations have additional wait time; have other things going on so that students always have something to do while their partners are finishing their portion of the project.
- Choose a communication tool. I suggest NiceNet's Internet Classroom Assistant (www.nicenet.org). Learn how to use it yourself, then introduce teacher partners to it. NiceNet is free but restricted to whomever you allow access, so it is very safe.
- Communicate often, even it is just to say, "We're still here."
- Start small; be faithful to your commitments.

Education Technology

Issues, Trends, and Leadership

Keil Hileman
Shawnee, Kansas

Many issues and challenges face public education today: funding, teacher retention and shortages, teacher education programs, school safety, a growing number of "at-risk" students, increased diversity of student needs, curricular alignment between states, and even a perception of teachers as nonprofessionals in our society. However, there is one challenge that stands out above all the others: the "information revolution" occurring globally as a result of new technologies. We are now in the Age of Information and Creativity.

The growth of the world knowledge base and development of new technologies have created the largest challenges public education has ever witnessed. Dr. Lawrence Roberts, one of the inventors of the Internet, points out, "the Internet doubles every six months, four times faster than transistors per each computer chip. . . . Creating an Internet medium which all other media will travel through by the year 2007." The leaps and bounds that our educational system has made in the last 100 years are very small compared to what we will have to do in the next 100 years. Most Americans are unaware that there is a tidal wave of information and technological change coming.

> While the Internet keeps growing, faster and larger, the number of users is also growing. When the number of users reaches saturation, the broadband width and high speed of the Internet will continue quadrupling each year, just like it has for the past 22 years. (Interview with Dr. Lawrence Roberts, available at http://www.ComputerUser.com)

John Kao of the Harvard Business School points out we are on the verge of a new age in human history; "we have gone from Agriculture to Industry to Information. Now we are entering the newest era: The Creative Age."

If you imagine our world is a river, then times of incredible change would be "rapids" or "white water" on the river. I believe we are in the middle of the Age of Information and witnessing the birth of the Age of Creativity. These amazing changes, or "white water," challenge us to continually improve our educational systems to meet emerging student needs. This is a time of constant change or "perpetual white water."

Education will need to become increasingly creative, flexible, and adaptable to help students become lifelong learners in an ever-changing world. At the same time, we still need to provide our students with a "base knowledge" of our culture and history. I believe we must focus on these curriculum outcomes: research and communication skills, critical thinking, teamwork, presenting, creativity, and information gathering and formatting.

Our students will need many skills to succeed in this Age of Information and Creativity. For the first time in history, we are seeing wealth created from information and creativity alone. The Microsoft Corporation was not founded on diamonds, gold, or land acquisitions but solely on creative ideas that allowed people to manipulate information in unique ways. Access to information allows people to succeed.

While technology connects the world in unique ways, our educational system must make every effort to keep students connected to, and prepared for, the real world. Permanent business and community relationships must be established to help schools attain these goals. Education and business partnerships will help schools fulfill their obligation to stay connected to technological changes and current life skills to insure future student success.

I am fortunate to work in a progressive district. We use the electronic service My Learning Plan (www.mylearningplan.com) to help organize and instruct our teachers and administrators. It allows me to share what I have learned with my peers. A teacher must simply fill out a presentation form and then present to the teachers who sign up for that session. However, the first step is to recognize the responsibility that every teacher has to share what we know not only with our students but with our colleagues as well. I have given many presentations on using computer programs, digital cameras, Internet research, and other topics.

The culmination of these teaching sessions was the development of a graduate-level course specifically designed for teacher recertification. The course I created is titled, "How to Turn Your Classroom Into a Museum." In this course I can reach teachers on many levels. We discuss artifact collection, organization, presentation, and use in the classroom. We also work with digital cameras, Internet research, Web page creation, digital scanners, and Microsoft Office. I feel obligated to teach this class and give inservice presentations. No one ever reached the spot where they stand today without the help of many people along the way. We must all find ways to share our talents and success with our colleagues and others in our educational communities.

Teacher education programs must be dedicated to teaching educators how to use current technologies and understand how they will apply to students' daily lives at home and on the job. The concept of being a lifelong learner must be fostered in professional educators and passed on to their students and surrounding communities.

The number of credits required for high school graduation increases each year, yet the number of student contact days rarely increases. Our school system adapted to meet the needs of agricultural communities by using spring break as a time to harvest hay or plant crops and late summer break as a time to harvest the majority of crops. The Information and Creative Age will require us to reorganize our academic years for increased time to motivate and educate.

The future that "perpetual white water" offers is unclear and uncertain. In the past, schools have been reactive in their attempts to change, leaving students behind. However, constant changes ahead may not allow us to predict and be proactive. I believe the answer may lie between being reactive and proactive. Education will have to stay connected to current technology. Staying current is not guessing about "what may be" or settling for "what was." It means working hard to use and learn from the technology and information that "is."

Education is not facing these challenges alone. Our nation, local businesses, neighboring nations, and every person around the world are facing the information tidal wave of technological change and the subsequent need to foster creativity. We must be forever vigilant in our search for creative and unique solutions to help us meet the educational needs of our students and prepare them for the society and world these changes will bring.

▨   Promoting Student Interest in Life Science and Technology by Making Students Active Learners

Lisa Alvey
West Paducah, Kentucky

Every year, as teachers await the return of the dreaded accountability testing scores, we share the same reactions: a queasy stomach, sleepless nights, the biting of the fingernails. Surely, we all have experienced disappointment when our students did not test as well as we thought they would and wondered, "What happened? I know they knew that!"

I have had these feelings many times and finally decided that I needed to come up with a plan. My stress level just couldn't take it year after year. This is how my story began.

It seems that one of our testing weaknesses, year after year, was in science and, of all things, life science. You would think that out of all the areas of science, life science would be the one all children would know the most about. After all, every elementary kid loves cute, cuddly little creatures. They all know a chicken comes from an egg and that if an animal's needs for food, water, and shelter are not met it will die.

Well, apparently we assumed they knew this, but the test scores showed otherwise. Each year I would expect the life science area to be the highest and it wasn't. In addition to the testing pressure, we live in a world that is advancing so fast in technology that it is hard to keep up.

These events are what brought on my desire to come up with a plan to develop hands-on activities for life science that would incorporate technology. After all, when we teach physical science, we bring out the wheels and pulleys. There had to be a way, short of establishing a zoo, to make life science more fun and to actively involve the students.

About the time my frustration with these problems became intolerable, I met a very enthusiastic gentleman by the name of Mr. Bill Freels, who was involved with the preservation of bluebirds in our area. He had a vision of setting up a bluebird trail on the school campus that included cameras. This would allow students to view activity in the nest on a monitor in the classroom. I liked the sound of this, and I decided that I would work with him. Maybe this would be a way to make concepts such as the life cycle, adaptations, and the food chain easier for my students to understand.

We began by purchasing a small camera similar to one that would be used in a home security system. It was mounted inside the top of bluebird nest box. It was then wired into the classroom so the students could watch "live action" on the monitor. We were fortunate to have birds showing an interest in the nest box the first week. Within two weeks, a pair of bluebirds had begun to construct a nest. We were all ecstatic about the images we were watching! They were beautiful and quickly became like our own pets. Over time, we watched as they built the nest and laid eggs. We continued to watch as the eggs hatched. We observed the male and female feed the young and remove the fecal sacks from the nest. We also watched as the babies grew and finally fledged. The day they left was a bittersweet day. We were like proud parents, yet probably felt like human parents feel when the last child leaves for college. I soon found that the students could relate many of our life science core content concepts to these bluebirds. It was finally real and they were actively involved as learners.

Our next project was to raise mealworms to feed our birds. (Now that is an up close and personal way to teach the life cycle!) Fourth graders who saw thousands of crawling mealworms thought it was about the most grotesque thing they had ever experienced, but they loved it! In our mealworm farm, all stages of the life cycle were present at all times. We built a small feeder and placed worms outside each day for our birds. After all, our babies needed a little help to locate food until they got the hang of it. This became a part of our studies of the food chain. I now had another core content concept they understood and could relate to from firsthand experience.

The following year, with a lot of help from many wonderful parents and family members, we set up a Web site where the children, their friends, and families could log on and watch the birds at home. This brought the technology into our project.

I am no technology wizard and I must admit I was a little unsure about taking this on, but I soon learned that many others felt that way. A number of e-mails and calls began to come in telling me that they could only view a black box. There was no picture. After several hours of investigating, I finally asked what time of day it was viewed. The answer to that question solved the problem. They were viewing it at night and didn't realize that when the sun went down, they would only see a black screen. I suddenly didn't feel so alone in the division of "computer challenged" people, and this gave me the confidence to continue. Before long, I had students who would answer questions that were e-mailed to us. Other students with interest in technology took on the job of investigating and resetting the computer when we had problems. It opened a whole new world of technology into my classroom.

During the second nesting season, we were approached by Cornell University's School of Ornithology. They were interested in hosting our bluebird cam. The exposure of the site through Cornell allowed us the wonderful opportunity to share the project with a much larger audience.

The word was now out and our e-mails began to come from all over the world.

After the first two years, I could see a definite rise in test scores and in the ability of the students to communicate their knowledge of life science concepts in discussions as well as in their writing. I felt the project had been a success, and there were many more core content concepts to teach. I only had to find a way to get my students more actively involved.

This brings me to the final phase (at least for now) of the plan. We are just completing a nature trail on the school campus. This was funded by a grant from Toyota along with many donations from local businesses and interested individuals. The trail is a mulched path that extends on three sides of the school and ends in an outdoor classroom. Along the trail we have approximately 20 stations to teach core content concepts from our science curriculum. These stations involve hands-on activities or real-life viewing of such things as erosion, succession, weather, animal habitats, martin houses, tree identification, native grasses, wild flower gardens, butterfly and hummingbird gardens, bat houses, a sand pit for viewing animal tracks, and an outdoor classroom that has a feeder watch station. None of this would be possible without community and business support. There are many grant opportunities available; the applications require a little time, but they are well worth the effort.

I am extremely excited about the future for our students and their science scores, but most of all, I am excited about the love and appreciation that the children are developing for the elements of nature that we all so often take for granted. Their test scores prove that they have a greater understanding of the concepts after participating in the program.

They have become actively involved learners rather than learning by reading facts in a book. This has encouraged me to venture into greater technology studies with the young children I teach. It has also shown me that there are many caring businesses and community members that are interested in the education of our youth. I find my students and I are more excited about learning than we were in the past. My greatest hope is that when these children grow up, they will remember what they have learned and will use that knowledge and the love they have for learning to teach others.

CHAPTER 4

Mentoring and Sharing Professional Development

 **Give Me an "H"**

Homework Strategies

Charla Bunker
Great Falls, Montana

Best practices for teacher leadership include motivating others to follow. As a National Board Certified Teacher, I have opportunities to motivate others by working as a state National Board facilitator, modeling teaching strategies, and mentoring beginning teachers. One way to motivate others to follow is to constantly strive to improve my own practice and be involved not only as an instructor in a community of learners, but also as a learner in that community. As an active learner, I motivate others to be community learners.

The No Child Left Behind Act has really influenced education, but not always in a positive manner. In a panic to inflate test scores, we are often driven to believe that more is better, especially in the area of homework. I certainly want my students to test well, but I do not believe that more is necessarily better. To confirm my beliefs, or be persuaded to change how I viewed the amount of homework students were assigned, I decided to enroll in an AFT Educational Research and Dissemination Program class. My goal was to learn what research proves is effective homework and align my homework practice with that research for the benefit of my students. My next goal would be to share this research with fellow teachers.

As a result of taking part in the Educational Research and Dissemination class, I learned that too much homework is as ineffective as too little homework. Ideally, homework should be assigned to extend the learning time of classrooms. The greatest effect of homework on student achievement occurs in high school. At my level, elementary, the effect of homework on student achievement is small, except for sustained home reading programs. It is suggested that 20 to 30 minutes per night for an elementary level student is the most effective. The purpose of homework should be to practice skills, to increase speed, to attain mastery or maintain skills, to increase participation of students in learning, to build student responsibility, to keep parents informed of what is happening in school, and to follow district policies. Homework should have a high success rate for students and not be used to teach complex skills.

In my classroom, I was proud of a 95% to 98% return rate on all homework assignments, but I wanted to reach all students and improve that rate to 100%. To do this, our school put two programs in place. First, if students do not turn in homework, they spend recess with me to complete it. If they miss more than three homework assignments in a quarter, they must enroll in a mandatory afterschool homework program. If parents have a problem with transportation, a bus provides students with a ride home. With these policies in place, homework return rates are now at 100%.

Research also states that feedback for student homework is vital. This is easily accomplished with assignments that are paper-and-pencil but not so easy to provide with assignments that do not include paper-and-pencil tasks, such as at home reading or studying for weekly spelling tests. Our school enacted a reading program for afterschool reading. All students are assigned 20 minutes of reading per night. Slips go home for parents or guardians to sign to validate the child's home-work reading. The slips are then collected and recorded the same as any other homework assignment.

Regarding studying for spelling tests, I decided to take a different approach. I explained to students that if they received a grade of less than a C on the test, I would be calling parents to make sure they were working. Calling parents was not as effective as I'd hoped, as many politely agreed to have their children study, but scores on final tests were not reflective of studying. Most of the children with failing grades attended the Boys and Girls Club. A simple call to the Boys and Girls Club education director solved this problem. The students have a Power Hour where they work on homework, and if they say they have none, they are allowed to watch educational videos. I explained that spelling words were assigned weekly and started fax-ing them to the director. I also explained that the students were expected to read for 20 minutes each day, and I sent reading slips to the Boys and Girls Club for the director to sign. The spelling scores improved dramatically, with no student achieving less than 80%. For one student, this studying improved her scores from 5% to 85%. I now communicate with the Boys and Girls Club education director at least once a week.

One routine with homework involved teaching a math lesson, allowing the students time to start the assignment at the end of class to show that they understood the concept, and then sending home what-ever part of the assignment they did not finish as math homework. According to research, this is not an effective use of homework time. Because math is a spiraling skill, it is vital that students remember what they learned previously to build on lessons they are currently learning. Effective homework for math includes reviewing previous assignments and allowing more time to complete the current assignment in class. If students do not finish the work in class, time after school with an instructor or helper can be helpful. Once again, this is because homework should be something that can be accomplished independently, and often, especially with math, students have questions.

This was a difficult homework strategy for me to change, but I wanted to give it a try. It also required me to sometimes assign less work on the current daily assignment. I was shocked and pleased by the results. Before changing my math homework practice, students were completing daily homework, but some students still failed the unit test, and the class average was 78%. After changing my homework practice, the class average rose to 88%, and not one student failed the test. I also had a parent of one of my gifted students comment at conference time that she was really pleased with how I was teaching math because her son was understanding math better than he ever had in the past. She was pleased that he was able to do the work independently. I was pleased to tell her that it was the homework policy that was working so well, rather than how math was being instructed. If she had not shared this information with me, I would never have realized that my previous homework policy was frustrating to parents.

For students to buy in to homework, they must have motivation. In our school, the homework reading slips provide a very old form of motivation, simple competition. With our fifth-grade classes, we post the number of reading minutes each class collects. The minimum time of reading is 20 minutes per night, but it is certainly not limited to 20 minutes. Students are motivated to turn in more. Another motivating factor for students is to have homework not just be busy work but designed with a purpose. Students also need feedback. Well-planned homework that gives students a feeling that they are making progress toward learning creates intrinsic motivation. It is my goal to someday have students beg for homework, chanting, "Give me an H, O, M, E, W, O, R, K: Homework!" I may dream outrageous dreams, but I truly believe that when we put forth our best practices in education, outrageous, wonderful things happen.

After attending the Educational Research and Dissemination class, I shared information with my colleagues in a college foundations class for new teachers that I teach at the local university. It has become my homework to spread the research on effective homework.

Helpful Tips

- It is vital to surround yourself with teachers who share a passion for teaching and are in education to make a difference in the lives of students.
- It is important to always be improving one's practice regardless of the number of awards or degrees one collects. Awards are wonderful, but the real reward in teaching is making a difference in students' lives each and every day.
- Being an educational leader is not always being the instructor. Educational leaders are also learners in the learning community.
- One would never go to a doctor who did not upgrade his or her skills, and students should not be expected to learn from a teacher who does not learn new teaching skills.
- Communication is key for effective teaching. This communication must occur with fellow educators, administrators, students, parents, community members, and policy makers.
- Public education is an outstanding value, and we need to let people know the positive attributes in our profession rather than dwell on problems.

▨ Team Teaching From Two Perspectives

Chris McAuliffe and Hillary Mason
White Lake, Michigan

When I was asked to write a chapter on teaming and leadership I thought the best way to look at it would be from all points of view. Currently I team teach with a rookie teacher. Because I am a veteran teacher with 17 years of experience, I figured that we would look at teaming in different ways. Hillary is in her second year of teaching and was my student teacher. We each sat down, wrote our thoughts about teaming, and then met to share them. I was surprised by the differences as well as the similarities. This is what we learned.

The Veteran's Point of View

Team or peer teaching has been around as long as I can remember. I have taught third grade and fifth grade and have successfully teamed at both levels. I team because it allows me to teach to my strengths and because I believe it gives our students the best environment for learning. I also team because I need the chance to bounce ideas off of somebody who looks at them from a fresh perspective. I have to admit that I also team for the companionship. Teaching can be a lonely profession. Many teachers spend their whole day in their rooms and never talk to other adults. Teaming provides me with an opportunity to talk with my partner daily about my successes and failures.

I team for obvious reasons, like teaching to strengths and making less work for each of us. But I also team because I have found that it enables us to provide our students with a much more consistent and balanced education. In fifth grade we believe in creating traditions. The fifth graders do everything together, instead of each class doing its own thing. We have our parties together; have Karaoke and Dance Revolution recesses. We use the same discipline plan and follow the same philosophy, and it travels from room to room. We go on field trips together and to camp together. We create a family atmosphere where all feel accepted. I believe this is accomplished because of the way we are teaming.

If teaming is to work, it must be the right makeup of teachers. Teams cannot be set up just because one person wants to teach math and another wants to teach science. The teachers must be compatible in teaching styles and discipline. I think too many teams are put together without truly looking at the makeup. I have been in situations where what is expected of the child and what the child can get away with vary from teacher to teacher. If you want to accomplish the kinds of things we do, this cannot happen. We tell our students at the beginning of the year that they will have more fun than any other fifth-grade class, but they will also work harder than any other fifth-grade class.

Once you have found somebody you are compatible with, the next step is realizing that this can be a lot of work. Many teachers approach teaming with the thought that it will make their jobs easier—and it does, in a lot of ways. However, it also creates more work in other ways. You must meet with your teammate(s) regularly and learn to make decisions that are best for the students. You must learn to make compromises for the best interest of the students. I am the kind of person who comes up with grand ideas and gets in way over my head. If I didn't have such a supportive team member, I couldn't do this. Hillary is always willing to do whatever she can to make my ideas come true even though this usually means more work for her.

Teaming has been especially helpful for me in ways that I wouldn't have expected. I have been teaching for many years and have won numerous awards. Yet I realize that it is nice to go to another teacher when I have an idea to get his or her input. Sometimes you just need to look at things from a different perspective. Our team has formed a strong and trusting relationship in which we feel comfortable giving each other input. I admire that a rookie teacher who student-taught with me is not afraid to stand up to me and tell me when she doesn't agree with something I am doing. It also impresses me that when I give her advice, she listens and realizes that I have been through everything she is going through and have helpful ideas. Teaming has allowed me to become an expert at what I do. I can concentrate on fewer things and try to master them. I also believe that the students see the teachers working together and learn from it.

The Rookie's Point of View

Teaching can be full of different stresses. Trying to fit the curriculum into the school year is tough enough without all the extras that come along with teaching. Individualized lessons, extra conferences, using technology, and teaching life skills are just a few of the expectations placed upon educators today. Teachers go into their classroom, close the door, and try to do it all. They feel a responsibility to teach everything perfectly. With so much that has to be taught each year, the need to cover all the material can contribute to burnout. One way to help alleviate this burden is team teaching.

When I started teaching I was lucky enough to have the opportunity to team with Chris, the other fifth-grade teacher in the building. We sat down and discussed our strengths in different aspects of the curriculum. Based on these talks, we decided to split subjects and specialize. We worked with our principal to set up a special schedule that would allow us blocks of time for our switches.

When we started teaming we taught our specified subjects. The stress was less, but still, the need to teach everything weighed heavily on me. As a new teacher, I spent hours after school trying to create the perfect units and lessons that would engage my students. Even though I was team teaching, I still felt the pressure to try to get everything done.

Then Chris and I started to overlap what we were teaching. He implemented strategies I taught in language arts into his science curriculum. I used Chris's science themes as the basis for writing topics in my class. The extra practice students received strengthened their skills. This, finally, alleviated some of my stress.

Chris and I also used the same discipline plan. This created a consistent environment for students. We were both involved in the structure of the plan and made sure the procedures were executed in the same way. Students knew what was expected in each classroom because the rules were clearly spelled out and students were held accountable.

Chris and I still talk multiple times a day. We discuss plans, student progress, behavior issues, and anything else that happens to arise during the course of a day. We plan fundraisers, fieldtrips, and units together. We split tasks so that one person is not taking on too much.

When we started team teaching I knew there would be many benefits. One benefit that I did not expect was the bonds between the students. They didn't have a classroom of peers to work and play with, they had two classrooms. Chris and I would open the wall between our rooms and have whole group discussions, activities, and parties. The students loved to form groups with their classmates from "the other side of the wall."

There was also a personal benefit to team teaching. I always have someone I can bounce an idea off of, which allows me to be more creative. Because Chris has taught for 17 years, he has a wealth of knowledge that I get to tap into. He can tell me what worked well for him, and what didn't, when I think about trying a new project or activity. Having another perspective helps me create better projects for my students.

Now don't misunderstand me, team teaching is not entirely a bed of roses. There are times when compromising is tough, and you can get on each other's nerves. But there is something very relaxing about knowing that you have someone at school who is always there to back you up and help you out. It's nice to have someone to assist with behavior issues, conferences, and paperwork. This takes away a lot of the stresses of teaching.

Our Discussion Wrap-Up

When we got together to discuss what we had written, we realized that we were teaming for different reasons. Even though we both believe that teaming is best for the students, our personal benefits are varied. However, whatever the reasons are, we both know that we are better off together. Teaming does take a lot of work, yet the rewards are endless.

Helpful Tips

- Find people that you are compatible with and enjoy working with. You will spend so much time with them that it needs to be a situation you enjoy. Convince your administration that you are the best team to put together; don't just let them place you.
- Don't team for the wrong reasons. This will create more work and you will be miserable.
- Remember when you are splitting subjects, projects, paperwork, and tasks that you need to rely on each other's areas of strength.
- Meet often with your team and give everyone a chance to give input. You need to have open communication almost daily. Remember that you are there to support, help, and laugh with each other.
- Realize that you will not always agree; there will be days when your partner drives you crazy. It happens to us too, and that is okay.
- Be consistent with discipline. This is a *must* for teaming.
- Don't be afraid to share what you are doing. Teachers tend to keep all of the wonderful things they are doing to themselves. Let the world know.
- Keep administration up to date on what your team is doing; you need their support.
- We can't stress enough the importance of keeping parents involved in what you are doing.

⧏ Enriching and Extending Teaching Through Professional Conferences

Deidre Austen
Lutherville, Maryland

A paradox exists in the classroom. Teachers spend most of their days with students only, effectively cut off from other adults and professionals. However, teachers are constantly being impacted by decisions made outside of the classroom by students' families, administrators, district leaders, state boards of education, and, ultimately, federal officials far removed from the learning environment. In order to manage what can become the isolation of the classroom, effective educators seek to nurture their professional development through continued education and seek productive ways to connect with their colleagues on both a personal and professional level. Attending professional conferences is an excellent way to accomplish the goal of staying connected to other adults while continuing to grow as educators. In this article, I offer advice for teachers attending professional conferences.

Top Ten Tips for Attending Professional Conferences

1. Identify Your Goal

Are you looking to improve your classroom management, learn new instructional strategies, identify methods for reaching reluctant learners, or extend your knowledge in a specific content area? Take time to reflect upon your personal and professional goals, as well as the stated goals of your school and district. Odds are, there is a conference out there that can address both your personal interests and your professional needs.

2. Choose a Conference That Truly Intrigues You

All teachers have experienced that painful moment when an audience has no interest in the content that is being presented; hopefully, less often when we are instructing than when we are members of that audience. When choosing a conference, make sure that you are interested and thus will be engaged in what is being presented.

Education supports myriad professional organizations that focus on learning disabilities, instructional practices, and specific content areas. Don't overlook workshops offered by publishers and other private businesses. Check with a variety of sources for recommended organizations, conferences, and workshops. Consider colleagues, administrators, district curriculum offices, and the Internet as resources. Teachnet is one of many services on the Internet that allows you to connect with teachers worldwide by e-mail through a moderated, filtered list (www.teachnet. com). Simply posting a query about worthwhile conferences will elicit a wide response. A small sampling of similar nationally recognized associations follows:

- National Council of Teachers of English: www.ncte.org
- International Reading Association: www.reading.org
- National Council of Teachers of Mathematics: www.nctm.org
- National Science Teachers Association: www.nsta.org
- International Society for Technology in Education: www.iste. org
- North American Association for Environmental Education: www.naaee.org

3. Seek Professional and Personal Support

Once you have identified a conference that you would like to attend, be sure that you have the support necessary to make the experience positive. If you have a family, is it reasonable for you to attend the conference? Do you have the resources to manage several days away, or should you plan to attend a local, one-day workshop? You will not benefit from your new learning if you are worried about your children getting on the bus, Junior getting to soccer practice, or the many other obligations that confront families daily.

As a bridge between the personal and professional, seek a colleague who might wish to attend the conference with you. There are few things more motivating than a supportive, enthusiastic fellow learner.

On a professional level, seek the support of your administration. Since you have already reflected on how the conference relates to school and district goals, share explicit ways that your students will benefit from your attendance at the conference. Explain how specific sessions fit into your existing curriculum. Express your willingness to share what you have learned so that other staff may also benefit from your new learning. This is an appropriate time to check on your district's policy about teachers' absences due to attendance at professional conferences. Ask about using professional days rather than your own personal days or leave.

4. Seek Financial Support

After obtaining your administrator's support, seek funding for your endeavor. Begin first by asking whether there are school funds to cover the entire expense of the conference. Some other sources for funding are your PTA, your district's curriculum office, and grants (though you will have to plan in advance for this option). If full funding is unavailable, ask for matching funds or for the cost of the conference itself. Consider joining the professional organization that is sponsoring the conference to save on the conference fee. This is also the time to check with your administration or district about the policy for transportation, meals, and lodging reimbursement. Be sure to ask whether receipts are necessary or whether a daily per diem reimbursement is used. Once your attendance has been approved, register online, if possible, to avoid standing in long lines at the conference.

5. Communicate With Your School Community

As the date of the conference approaches, share your plans with your school community. If you work with multiple teachers in a support role, explain what you hope to gain from the conference and how you have planned to meet your responsibilities while you are away. If a substitute will be provided, share the substitute's name and the plans that you have provided. Just as you share your plans with your colleagues, share with the other partners in your students' education—the students themselves and their families. Again, explain which qualified substitute will be teaching while you are away. Include details about specific sessions that you will attend and your enthusiasm about sharing your new knowledge with your students when you return.

Continue to communicate as you plan the sessions you wish to attend at the conference. Most national organizations will publish session descriptions ahead of time that you can use to schedule your conference. Ask colleagues whether there are specific topics that interest them. Check with your principal about sessions that will support school goals. Consider contacting district curriculum offices to ascertain whether new units are being developed or old ones revamped. These early efforts will help you focus your schedule and ensure relevant new learning.

6. Pack Thoughtfully

Several helpful items to bring to the conference:

- *Self-stick notes.* For taking notes and recording reflections.
- *Folders for organizing handouts and resources.* It makes filing and sharing much easier when you return to school.
- *Address labels preprinted with your name, school address, phone number, and e-mail.* Makes sharing professional information with vendors, presenters, and fellow attendees more expedient.
- *Calculator*
- *Briefcase or backpack.* If vendors attend the conference, you will have many opportunities to pick up catalogs and freebies.
- *Comfortable shoes.* Many national conferences have sessions spread out among several hotels or convention centers; you may walk several miles a day.
- *Bottled water and snacks.* Food and beverages are generally available, but you will be able to stick to your schedule (and budget) and keep your energy up if you bring your own water and healthy snacks.
- *Reading material.* There will undoubtedly be time to read when you have just finished a session but the next one does not begin for 20 minutes.
- *Cell phone.* Invaluable for keeping in contact if attending with a colleague.

7. Get the Most out of the Conference, Without Becoming Overwhelmed

Having put so much into planning this opportunity, you could easily fall into the mentality of needing to fill every moment of the conference with sessions and take advantage of every offering—don't. Burning out will defeat the purpose of attending a conference to rejuvenate your teaching. As you look over the schedule and plan your days, note the location of sessions and take into account the time needed to get from one location to another. Also note alternate sessions in the same location in case a workshop that you wish to attend is full. Many presenters will offer their handouts for a small fee at a central copying location; this is an option if you have a conflict and truly wish to receive information on a topic.

Schedule breaks within your day, keeping in mind your own energy level and needs. Attending three to four sessions a day is manageable; attending five to six sessions daily is not. If you are traveling with a colleague, consider attending separate sessions and sharing handouts. During your breaks, organize the materials that you have received in the folders that you packed.

Keep track of the sessions you attend and the time that you spend at vendors. Many organizations will notarize a record of professional development hours for the time that you spend at the conference.

8. Take Full Advantage of Vendors and Display Areas

Most regional and national conferences are inundated with publishers and a plethora of educational supply companies. Vendors often offer free materials ranging from catalogs to lesson plans to instructional material. This is a great place to pick up "goodies" to share with your colleagues and students. If you listen to demonstrations, you may be offered complimentary classroom supplies. Check with vendors to find out whether they are organizing any focus groups. By attending a focus group, you may be provided with lunch and vouchers for educational materials. It can be well worth your time.

9. Share When You Return

Share with your colleagues informally by e-mailing new information or Web sites, showering them with freebies, and offering ideas at faculty meetings. Share on a more formal level with presentations at staff development days and by communicating your willingness to work with the district curriculum office. When you incorporate new strategies or materials into your lessons, be sure to share with your administration, parents, and students that you learned these ideas at the recent conference. This will make the benefits of the time away from the classroom evident to the entire school community. Use your enthusiasm to encourage colleagues to also attend conferences.

10. Reflect Upon Your Conference Experience

As you file away your new resources, contemplate the sessions you attended. Which were the most beneficial? Why were these sessions such positive experiences? If you have contact information, let the presenters know your thoughts. They may have material to share or may contact you in the future as they develop additional presentations. What strategies did the presenter use that made your new learning meaningful and engaging? Keep these thoughts in mind; the day may come when you are presenting and helping others as they pursue their own professional growth.

Leading and Modeling Staff Development Initiatives Within Faculty Groups and Within the School

Frank Rossi
West Haven, Connecticut

Teachers are constantly searching for ways to provoke interest and initiative in our classes. We dream up creative lesson plans or develop hands-on projects or programs in an attempt not only to develop our students' skills but also to capture and maintain their interests in what, to them, can often be dull and boring material. In the brief time that I have been teaching at the high school level, I learned quickly that we need to be as much an entertainer as we are a facilitator. Black and white textbooks are being replaced by laptop computers, high-definition television, and multimedia presentations. In this age of the Internet and technology, teachers need to be taught that their role is changing from the "sage on the stage" instructor to that of a cofacilitator working alongside students, guiding them to meet the goals we set for them. One of my most important goals regarding professional development is to learn new ways to keep my material and techniques fresh and innovative. So why does it seem that so many professional development situations teach us using the very same methods we are encouraged *not* to use in our own classrooms?

I can recall one of the very first professional development classes I attended as a new teacher—"Making a Classroom Web Site Work for You and Your Students." I found myself in a hotel conference room with about 30 other teachers taking notes from a PowerPoint presentation. The only computer in the room was used to display information through a projector. We spent the morning being "talked at" and given rules, lists, and some ideas. For the first time as a teacher, I put myself in the seat of some of my students, realizing how boring it must be to listen to someone for 40 to 60 minutes at a time. Even in classroom conversation, more than half the students are not actively participating. I left that conference with a pile of paperwork but no real idea of how to create this Web site, nor any realization of the workshop's goals. In fact, to this day I am not totally sure what those goals were. I learned much from the workshop—not about Web design or site planning, but that I need to spend less time in front of the classroom and more time *in* the classroom.

As a teacher of technology, I have been asked to initiate staff development in our school and surrounding schools regarding the use of basic computer technology such as presentation software, Web design, and word processing. When planning a workshop I try to create an environment that would be similar to a typical classroom. Given the choice, many students would rather not be in school so we must make it "worth their while" and interesting. I am sure there are many teachers who would rather not attend professional development workshops or seminars for many of the same reasons students do not want to be in school; they are dull, boring, and often ineffective. My goal is to make my sessions worth the participants' while, whether it is a brief one- or two-hour session or a full day.

The first step is to set a goal. This goal should be something that can be realized by the end of the session and must be tangible. I don't believe that "learning how to set up a Web-guided lesson" is as effective a goal as "*completing* a Web-guided lesson." Develop some type of project or assignment that can be completed in the time allowed. My goal is to have teachers leave one of my workshops with a finished, tangible product that can be applied to their classes and used with their students the very next day.

We often leave professional development workshops with a wealth of new ideas, only to file them away in our memories and eventually lose track. How many times have you thought to yourself, "That's a great idea; I should use that sometime!" Then that "sometime" never comes. With the workshop's main objective in mind, I plan to create an environment in which teachers can put the new ideas to use *during* the workshop. Instead of trying to determine when they can incorporate these new ideas, they leave the workshop already having done so.

After determining a goal, the next most important aspect of organizing a professional development workshop is to plan for your participants to come prepared. If your goal is to have teachers leave with a tangible, immediately usable, ready-to-implement product, then they must come with the tools necessary to put it all together. It might be an older lesson or assignment plan, or it could be an entire unit's worth of resources. It could even be handwritten lecture notes or an older sample of student work. The more information your participants have with them, the more productive they can and will be. This will also prevent them from losing track of information that they might want to save for later in the term.

One of the most overused pieces of software, in my opinion, is PowerPoint or any other presentation software. Often, as a student in a workshop, I find myself reading slides and not paying attention to the instructor. When using presentation software, I believe *less is more.* Use the presentations for examples, key words, or pictures. Again, I have a "practice what you preach" mentality to these workshops. We would all be very upset if our students ignored us because all of our notes were on PowerPoint, yet we all do exactly the same thing at professional development workshops. Create handouts in which your audience can fill in blanks as you feed them information. Do not give it to them all at once on a screen.

Three years ago my school began an initiative to promote teacher-created Web sites. New software was purchased and development workshops were planned. Nearly half the faculty members signed up to take these workshops on Web design. We discussed what should be included, how they could be set up, and basic Web design principles. For four days teachers came to the computer lab and practiced making Web sites. The goal of this workshop was to instruct teachers at our school how to use the Web design software. Every teacher left the workshop excited to experiment. Everybody had great ideas. Then the school year started and all of those ideas were put on hold. After a couple of months, I would get many questions concerning some the concepts that were "forgotten." Two years passed and not one faculty Web site existed.

At the beginning of this past school year, another push was made for faculty members to create some type of presence on the Web. We started with five teachers. This time, each teacher was asked to bring materials that he or she would want to publish on the Web, materials such as notes, assignments, presentations, Web links, and calendars. By the end of the week, each teacher had a Web site ready to publish. Midway through the year, a similar workshop was offered to more teachers. Nearly a dozen teachers took part, and after one full-day workshop they all had something that could be published. The difference between this year and three years ago was the goal. Teachers were asked to come prepared to this workshop, were told they would use the material they brought with them, and they left with the finished product ready for implementation. Nobody did anything just for the sake of doing something.

Our goal as teachers is to encourage our students to be lifelong learners in every aspect of their lives and careers. Shouldn't we model the goals we set for them? Why does there seem to be a different set of rules when teaching teachers how to teach? As we progress through our own careers, keeping up to date with new material is a "given." As times change, so should our techniques and methods.

Helpful Tips

- Consider your audience. Be sure this workshop will be "worth their while." Don't just plan arbitrary sessions.
- Be specific when stating your goals. Be sure to set a goal that can be realized and ready to implement the very next day.

- Design your session around some type of project that your participants must complete. Everyone should leave the session with something tangible.
- As a facilitator, you should not be doing all the work while the participants just sit and listen. Participants should have hands-on objectives to complete, planned and designed prior to the session.
- Prepare your audience ahead of time. They should come prepared with materials to apply toward your goal.
- When using presentation software, remember *less is more.* Limit the words on your slides. Use overheads and projectors to demonstrate graphics or examples.

Developing Interest in Reading Strategies Inside the Teaching Community

Jonathan Kern
Jacksonville, Florida

As a school standards coach, I work with teachers on developing instruction that allows students to reach the standards set forth by the Florida Department of Education. I have decided to tackle the job by showing teachers how to use reading strategies in their classrooms regardless of the content they are teaching.

I began the year by developing a reading assessment that I wrote on each grade level, from 6 to 12. The questions were modeled after our state standardized test. They followed the same pattern with regard to question type (e.g., main idea, author's purpose, point of view) regardless of the grade level the student would be completing. This allowed teachers to easily complete an item analysis of the assessment in order to determine the most deficient skill areas of their students. After those deficiencies had been determined, I searched for strategies that would target those deficiencies in order to give the teachers a way to deal with the information given to them by the assessment.

Once I found the strategies, I scheduled days to meet with the teachers to explain the natural progression of assessment, analysis, and planning in order to show them how to change their style of teaching and attend to deficient reading skills. Teachers picked strategies they felt would work best for their students and developed their lessons, regardless of content, using those strategies. Teachers were very receptive to switching their styles from content-based education to strategy-based after they read the data resulting from the item analysis. By allowing teachers to see clearly how this sort of plan is laid out, there was more buy-in to it than to programs from the past.

In addition, I picked four main strategies to target the four strands of reading comprehension on our state's standardized test. The strategies were given to and modeled for social studies and science teachers. Teachers teach one of these strategies per week until the students are familiar with the strategies, at which time they are divided into groups by their deficiency areas. Then, regardless of content, students will be able to follow these strategies with a partner to read new textbook information and make sense of it. Teachers are excited to use the strategies and to differentiate the instruction in the manner in which it has been explained to them. Again, this excitement for teaching reading strategies was generated by teachers looking at data and then being able to see trends they can attack by teaching in a manner with which they were not familiar.

In addition to attempting to generate excitement inside the classroom, I also have organized and facilitated a book tournament at a local Barnes and Noble bookstore over the past few years. I recruit four local middle schools to provide teams of five students who answer questions about a classic book (*To Kill a Mockingbird, The Giver, Fahrenheit 451,* to name a few) in a game-show format. The local newspaper, the *Florida Times Union,* provides a reporter to serve as the master of ceremonies. He or she also provides the questions that will be asked of the students. Barnes and Noble provides the comfortable venue and prizes and awards for the winners. The media helps to generate excitement by providing information to the public about the tournament.

This year, students on the teams will be required to run book drives at their respective schools in order to collect new and used picture books to donate to Barnes and Noble's holiday book drive program for children in need. So, the students will get the chance to flex their reading muscles and give back to their community. The tournament generates excitement about reading in each of the involved schools and will hopefully provide hundreds of young children the opportunity to become more interested in reading at a younger age. In addition to getting children involved, the teachers who sponsor the teams for the individual schools get to experience the reading process from a different perspective by teaching reading skills to students who are motivated by pure competition.

Helpful Tips

- As an instructional leader, it is easier to provide professional development opportunities when you have data to back up your instruction. Teachers will find it much more appealing when they have a true reason for trying something new.
- Teachers find it even more appealing when someone else does all the planning for them in order for it to happen in the classroom.

Teaching Is Not a Solitary Profession

Laura Partridge
Arlington, Virginia

There never seems to be enough time in the day for teachers. There is always another lesson to plan, paper to grade, student to help, parent to call, or meeting to attend. As such, it is easy to be reluctant to set a time to meet with other teachers when it is not required. However, I have found that interacting with other teachers ultimately is a time saver and helps make all teachers involved in the collaboration more effective.

Many school districts, including my own, have formal mentoring programs. These programs typically pair a veteran teacher with a new teacher or new hire to the school district. For new teachers, it is invaluable to have the insight of an experienced teacher. Formal mentoring programs help ensure that new teachers have a veteran teacher who is dedicated to helping his or her mentee in a nonjudgmental way to answer any questions and to learn the nuances of the school. It seems intuitive that the mentee benefits; however, the mentor also learns from the new teacher. I have yet to mentor a teacher who has not provided me with some strategies or insights that have helped me become a more effective teacher.

Another idea is to collaborate with colleagues on teacher research. I am currently involved with several other math teachers working on our professional development plan. We decided to work together because we had a common concern about the poor passing rate of special education students on the state math test for eighth graders. Passing a certain number of state tests is required for graduation, so the stakes for the students are high. We meet regularly and are in the process of developing a plan to deliver instruction and provide regular assessment of key areas that consistently have given our school's students difficulties. Since all the special education math teachers in our school are involved, we can develop a progressive plan so that students in resource math are receiving instruction that complements and builds on itself from grade to grade as we target the identified curricular areas. Our meetings also give us time to share ideas and strategies for teaching concepts or for helping a particular student.

Co-planning is a strategy that I was reluctant to try. I always assumed that it would be too time restrictive because it would require me to meet regularly with other teachers at school. I also assumed that it would take longer to plan with others than it would by myself. However, a colleague convinced me to try it, and I'm now a believer. When you are establishing a co-planning relationship, it will take more time as you work out the logistics. However, co-planning ultimately saves time on the administrative tasks as you share the responsibility of copying worksheets or creating and modifying tests. In addition, you have continual access to another teacher's pedagogical ideas and resources, which can help you co-create a richer lesson plan. The dialogue that occurs with the other teacher, both during planning and after the lesson, also provides insight into ways to improve your teaching. Co-planning gives you a chance to debrief and reflect with another teacher, something that rarely happens otherwise.

If you are reading this book, then you obviously are interested in continuing your own professional development as you strive to become a more effective teacher. Teaching should not be a profession in which you compete against other teachers; rather, it should be a profession in which you work cooperatively with other teachers. Many teachers use published material to help in the classroom and think nothing of it. However, teachers often are reluctant to ask colleagues for ideas, as if that was somehow cheating. It's not. Dialogue with other teachers is an underutilized and powerful resource. So, become a mentor, do collaborative research, or co-plan. You'll be glad you did.

▧ Professional Development

A Life-Changing Event

Linda Antinone
Fort Worth, Texas

My life changed in 1991 after I attended a two-week workshop that transformed my philosophy of teaching. When I was selected to attend CalcNct, a national program sponsored by the Department of Education, I never expected to begin a new life, but I did.

As a math and science education major at the Ohio State University, I learned early on about the need for continued professional development. John Novak, a science education professor, encouraged us to attend the state science teachers' meeting and then the National Science Teachers of America meeting during my junior year. I learned that effective teaching requires a commitment on the part of the teacher to continue to learn and improve. I saw enthusiastic veteran teachers share effective teaching strategies and activities. These experiences helped me to understand that I was beginning a vocation, not just a job.

As a beginning teacher in Cincinnati and then Columbus, I attended local and state meetings for mathematics and science teachers. As a novice, I needed the voices of experience and found many teachers who were willing to share effective strategies. I found that informal conversations were as helpful as the formal sessions that I attended. In Columbus, the local mathematics and physics teachers met at least once a year to share teaching strategies. I was a beginner, so I attended mostly to learn and gather materials. As I gained experience, I found myself contributing to the sessions more and more.

In 1989, Greg Foley, a professor at Ohio State University, began a local group for calculus teachers on the use of graphing calculators to teach calculus. These sessions met several times over a two-year period and were focused on training teachers to learn about new technologies. By 1991, Dr. Foley had moved to Texas and received a grant to train teachers to use graphing calculators. Having been a member of his group in Columbus, I decided to apply. At 29, I was the youngest of the 35 teachers accepted nationally.

The mathematics problems and strategies in the CalcNet workshop challenged me to change my way of teaching and thinking. Students were going to be using graphing calculators with powerful software to explore and discover concepts. I was to give more control over to the students and let them develop mathematical ideas. While this was scary, I found myself exploring new ideas and understanding them better than I had previously. I shared these new ideas with students and found that they were as excited as I was. Students began asking different questions. They could visualize mathematics and ask higher level questions. This presented another challenge for me because I was not always able to answer the questions immediately.

In Columbus, another teacher and I began a local area CalcNet to share ideas with other teachers in central Ohio. The national CalcNet grant had required us to go back and train teachers in our own area. I had never given a training session and was scared, but because it was required, I felt obligated. I conducted sessions not only for mathematics teachers but also for physics teachers in our area. I was using technology with students and saw how much they were learning from these new methods. I began writing my own activities and communicating with my CalcNet colleagues to share ideas and lessons. I was hooked, and before I knew what was happening, I found myself presenting sessions to audiences at the state and national levels.

I began collaborating with other teachers excited about the use of technology in the classroom and developed a one-week workshop, Connecting Math and Science, in 1994 with two other teachers. This workshop brings together mathematics and science teachers to learn how to collect data with probes like temperature, motion, and light and analyze it from both the mathematical and scientific perspectives. The program provides many activities that are ready to use but also requires teachers to develop a lesson with a small group and share it with the whole group. This workshop is now a part of the professional development program offered by Texas Instruments called Teachers Teaching with Technology (T[3]). The T[3] program is a group of teachers who use technology effectively with students and share their ideas with other teachers. An important part of the program is the fact that classroom teachers are teaching other classroom teachers with materials developed and tested by classroom teachers.

My life since CalcNet '91 has changed dramatically. I have become a teacher dedicated to helping all students succeed in mathematics through the use of techniques that motivate and actively involve them in discovering and understanding mathematical concepts. This is in contrast to the methods I previously used when I presented all information to students and allowed them to be successful by practicing skills without necessarily understanding concepts.

My experiences in attending and presenting professional development activities have taught me several things. First, professional development comes in many different forms. It can be local in a school or district, formal, or informal. It can also take place in local areas or at the state and national levels. Second, we must all get involved and help each other to develop better methods of teaching. I find that I must continue to look for good lessons and analyze what I learn to see what works best with my personality, skill level, and knowledge. I cannot always simply take what is in a book or what I learned at a workshop and teach it without thinking. I must think about my students and the resources we have available at my school. I must continually analyze what I do, think about why I do it, and reflect on the results through student assessments. Professional development, whether it is sharing ideas with a colleague next door, attending a national meeting, or reading a professional journal, is essential for me to be the best teacher that I can be and for my students to be as successful as they can be. We all need to continue to learn and grow as teachers. The future of our students depends on it.

Helpful Tips

- When students are actively involved in meaningful activities, they learn. Finding activities that engage students and promote higher level thinking is a challenge. These lessons are not always found in teacher editions of textbooks. These lessons are developed through thoughtful analysis and continued professional development.
- Talk to the other teachers in your building. Don't be afraid to ask for help. Teaching is challenging every day, but especially during the first few years. Ask successful teachers whether you can observe them teach a class, plan together, or give you some helpful tips for the challenges that you face.
- Discussion groups in a school that focus on effective teaching strategies promote success for students. The mathematics department at my school holds its own professional development sessions. We analyze school test data along with an examination of test questions with our student answers, discuss strategies for improving performance of students, train each other on technology, share lessons, and develop new lessons to encourage cooperative learning. Cooperative learning activities encourage students to work together in small groups to achieve a goal. The situation works best when each member is forced to be an active participant and must contribute to the solution.
- Get involved in the teaching organizations in your local area or state. Many national and state organizations need volunteers during conferences. This is a great way to meet other talented teachers in your field. Look for opportunities

to volunteer, or e-mail organization leaders to ask about opportunities to help out.

- Join national organizations in your field, and attend national meetings when you can. The professional journals that you receive contain many great teaching ideas. The National Science Teachers Association offers reduced rates for new teachers during their first three years in the profession. Check your professional organization to see whether they offer specials when you are a new teacher. Most offer schools the opportunity to join as an organization, which allows teachers access to professional journals and resources without requiring individual membership from each person. This is especially useful in elementary schools where teachers teach many subjects.
- Build your own library of resources including professional journals, resource books, materials from conferences, and lessons that you develop. Keep them organized so that you can find material when you need it.

CHAPTER 5

Teaching With Passion

⧖ **Leading Through Excitement**

Tammy Haggerty Jones
Sauk Village, Illinois

I see the world through the eyes of a child. I believe that the world is filled with wonder, that learning is exciting, and that anything is possible with a little imagination, tape, string, glitter, and a box of crayons.

In Room 13, I teach the children that it is acceptable (and encouraged) to take risks, make mistakes, get messy, giggle, and have fun in the process. I promote a community environment that is nurturing, loving, creative, and forgiving.

As you walk down the third-grade corridor to the last classroom on the right, you can't help but notice that something exciting is happening both inside and out. As you cross the threshold into our room, a magical transformation occurs. Each month I imaginatively connect the Illinois Learning Standards, our district curriculum, and a project-based monthly theme.

Our December theme was "Sweet Home Chicago." I learned that only four of my 23 students had ever been to the city, and I was determined to bring Chicago to Room 13. Fifty-three phone calls later, the Windy City arrived at my door. Box loads of promotional materials and gifts arrived, to the amazement of wide-eyed children ready to learn.

We experienced a "Taste of Chicago" (an annual lakefront festival) by dining in Chicago's most popular restaurants, complete with tablecloths, menus, music, and money math problems. The children recreated the Museum of Science & Industry's holiday tree display and decorated three classroom trees with handmade ornaments from India, Mexico, and Japan.

We toured Adler Planetarium and posed for pictures in front of the solar system dressed in bright orange spacesuits. My students also participated in a classroom version of the Lincoln Park Zoo's "Caroling to the Animals" annual event. My students donned elephant, gorilla, giraffe, lion, and tiger costumes and paraded around the room while singing Christmas carols to a group of preschoolers. The children created cubist self-portraits after visiting the Picasso exhibit at The Art Institute of Chicago. They also created murals similar to those created by Diego Rivera after visiting The Mexican Fine Arts Museum.

A favorite class activity was singing in our classroom during lunch. In order to sing "Go, Cubs, Go," "Sweet Home Chicago," and 43 other Chicago-based tunes, the children had to read the printed lyrics. The unit ended with a guest speaker from Marshall Fields sharing the history of the department store through a collection of artifacts, recreating the famous clock out of construction paper and glue, and assembling gift baskets filled with delicious Frango Mint chocolates.

I create adventures for my classroom because the majority of my students have never experienced the culture around them. Museums, skyscrapers, theatre, restaurants, festivals, and the lakefront are within a 40-minute drive. Field trips are not permitted, so I apply for grants and invite museums and speakers to come to the school. We take imaginary field trips and dress up in costumes that I find at post-Halloween clearance sales.

We do not have an art department, a playground, or a budget for classroom supplies, so I ask local merchants to donate specific items for my students. In return, my students and I send thank you notes and photographs of our learning activities to our benefactors.

Federal funding or a classroom budget would be nice, but we have something more valuable than gold. We have our imaginations!

My students were greeted on the first day of school with a "Strassburg Spelunkers" opening theme. The idea came to me while my family and I were on an adventure vacation to the caves and caverns of southern Indiana and northern Kentucky. We took walking tours and admired the stalactites and stalagmites, sailed in a glass-bottomed boat and looked for blind crayfish, and panned for gemstones. I even suited up in "cave gear" and participated in a two-hour wade, climb, and crawl. I took my philosophy of "take risks, get messy, and giggle" to a whole new level. I knew that if I were excited about teaching, they would be excited about learning!

From there, my head started spinning with ideas. I went to my local public library and checked out 40 books about caves, caverns, rocks, minerals, and bats. I collected samples of rocks and minerals found in caves and hid obsidian, amazonite, calcite, limestone, citrine, and rose quartz inside my classroom sand table. The children were then able to sift, pan for treasures, and chart their findings in a journal and on a map.

We transformed our room into the Marengo Caves and Bluespring Caverns by making stalactites, stalagmites, pillars, and columns. We hung the formations all around our room and used rulers to measure and calculate the age of each one. Silver and gold glitter was added to give the formations extra sparkle, and a few bats were hung upside down from the ceiling for authentic representation and for plain old fun.

The children and I watched videos about caves, wrote creative stories, painted rocks to represent gemstones, read the book *Mystery of the Cave,* added new vocabulary to our Word Wall, and completed a 16-page Spelunker's Journal as an alternative assessment. The highlight of our unit came when we borrowed a tunnel from the preschool, made construction paper headlamps, turned off the lights, and simulated an actual crawl. Each child received a digital picture of his or her adventure. Their smiles were priceless.

I know my students are experiencing success when they make personal connections between the textbooks, our themes, and life experiences. They are actively engaged in learning, so positive interpersonal relationships result and inappropriate behavior is rare.

I can see the twinkle in their eyes when they bring in rocks found on the way to school and hold them out to me with pride. Our cave unit was back in August, and my students are still looking for cave and mineral books in the library at school.

I applied for a grant through the Field Museum of Chicago and was able to provide 250 third-grade students with the opportunity to experience the Soil Adventure Mobile, an outreach program designed to complement the museum's "Underground Adventure" exhibit. As the children rotated from center to center, I could hear them engaging in conversations with the museum educators. At one station, the children tested soil samples taken from our school, held the elements in outstretched hands, and determined which type of soil they had. One of my students asked whether the soil sample he was holding was similar to that found in a cave. He made a connection. He took ownership. He found power in knowledge.

When I arranged for the John G. Shedd Aquarium outreach program to come to our school, another of my students was thrilled when he made the connection that bats in a cave use echolocation similar to that used by a dolphin in the ocean. He learned about bats back in August. The children were still making Shedd Aquarium connections when it came to our "Sweet Home Chicago" unit in December.

Our September unit was called "Our Amazing Ocean." During July, I participated in a "Wild Reef" three-part series of workshops at the John G. Shedd Aquarium in Chicago. I was so excited after learning about seahorses, sharks, and coral that I spent the rest of the summer preparing the unit. My family joined in on the fun. We enjoyed spending time at the aquarium, reading books, gathering shells, and preparing for my students' adventure.

Earlier that summer, I met a teacher at a Science, Nature & Art workshop who taught in one of Chicago's most affluent suburbs. She won a sand table at a silent auction and had no use for it in her classroom. She generously gave it to me, and it became the focal point of our sand and shell exploration lessons.

I contacted a national retail chain and asked them to donate clearance beach towels, tropical fish posters, paperback dictionaries, plastic tablecloths, and a globe. They did, and they gave me more than I asked for. I also contacted a local grocery store and asked for food donations so the children could "Dine Out on a Coral Reef" in a series of hands-on activities that I learned at the Shedd Aquarium workshops.

I also brought in 30 plastic fish plates to hold base ten blocks, 27 plastic fish and dolphin toys to be used as writing buddies, and a 10-foot-long wooden wave that I found in the garbage. My students benefited through the generous donations of others.

Throughout the month-long unit, I was in contact with my instructors at the Shedd Aquarium. We shared strategies and lessons designed for the third-grade learner. I sent them photographs and samples of our work. I met with my principal and arranged for the Shedd Aquarium to come to our school and present a "Voices from the Amazon" outreach program for the entire third grade and for the eight autistic children in the SPEED Center.

I met with the eight other third-grade teachers and with my graduate student teacher from St. Xavier University to develop pre-visit activities for the children. The third graders read stories, wrote essays, and located the rainforest on a map. On the day of the presentation, you could feel the excitement in the air. The halls were decorated with tropical fish, shark, seahorse, dolphin, and whale research reports. Uniform shirts were properly tucked into navy blue pants, hair was combed, teeth were brushed, and the children displayed their best "company manners." The Wild Reef team would be arriving soon. The children were ready for their learning adventure.

The highlight of the day was when each child and teacher was presented with a free family pass to the aquarium. The monetary value of the pass alone equaled a week's grocery bill or a month of electric service. The educational value of the pass was priceless. The children could see, up close, all of the creatures we learned about in class.

Since the presentation in September, the third-grade team has been energized. Six of us participated in a "Voices of the Amazon" workshop at the aquarium. We drove to Chicago together, spent the day learning and playing, created lessons for our rainforest unit, shopped in the gift store until we ran out of hands, and found greater respect for each other.

Amazing things happen when you teach from the heart. People respond. Children learn.

▨ Peeking Through My Door

Maria Jose De la Torre
Pineville, North Carolina

> The mediocre teacher tells.
> The good teacher explains.
> The superior teacher demonstrates.
> The great teacher inspires.
>
> —*William A. Ward*

Outstanding teaching usually rumbles in the hallways when a classroom door is opened. Allowing teachers to look at what is happening inside a colleague's classroom can be a learning encounter without precedent. In my experience, modeling has been the most effective way to reach my fellow teachers, and I, too, have learned more from observation than from most of the workshops and lectures that I have attended. I am convinced that there are actions that cannot be articulated in words, only witnessed and reproduced.

Like cooking recipes, teaching techniques have been analyzed "scientifically" or handed over "home made." As a result of research and long hours of careful thought, specific teaching methods have been published and have empowered many teachers all around the world. However, much more has been learned in sessions with "grandma teachers" where the extraordinary has been revealed. Underlying extraordinary teaching is the common sense modus operandi: passion for teaching. Even though passion for teaching has worked since teachers were teachers, such a subjective matter, where plans and procedures can be difficult to describe, can only be taught through modelling.

In my educational psychology thesis, I analyzed the passion for teaching as an intangible element that has often been displaced from the research lens by the quest for step-by-step plans that everyone could follow. Monitoring teachers who had a special passion for teaching, as indicated by their students, I came to realize that much could be learned from a teacher's enthralled spirit and how the reflection of that inner reverence for knowledge awakes a true learning hunger in a student. Modelling was the cornerstone: seeing that there is a human being who is so passionate about knowledge, and who is so passionate about revealing it to others, made even the most apathetic agree that there must be something worthwhile to be considered. Along those same lines, it was easy to conclude that teachers could also absorb this fervor for teaching by watching passionate teachers perform and becoming infatuated with their own profession.

Such conclusions set in motion an engine in my teaching profession that I have zealously kept running. I examined carefully those teachers who inspired me, who were able to launch my teaching higher, and I tried to imitate their ways. I learned how to grow enchanted by language arts, by science, by social studies, and by math. I learned the meaning of being a lifelong learner with a sincere veneration of knowledge, and I learned how my teaching style had to become more vulnerable to my inner curiosity. I found myself stimulating my best thinking, invigorating my spirit, and testing my courage in the classroom. I realized that teaching is a deeply personal relationship with the world of knowledge and that it required that I would impart this affection to my students.

My lessons became vibrant adventures; like an actor on stage, my voice and movements were enough to pop out my students' eyes. I would stand on a chair, crawl like a baby, or laugh like an old lady, just like a storyteller who had no other tools. Once a student told me that I taught as if it were the last time I would teach! I had discovered the humor and playfulness of teaching to spark the true inquisitiveness of learning. In that same spirit, I began to bring in gadgets, animals, costumes, and all sorts of objects, allowing my imagination to run free and, most importantly, my students' as well. I became skillful at balancing the curriculum with my teacher's soul, the must-do's with the want-to-do's, and I began to cook contents and skills with many more spices and condiments. My classrooms turned into colorful African jungles, business strip malls, or buildings in flames. I spent my time decorating the walls, the doors, and the ceiling while the state test scores were soaring to the top. There was no other explanation: students were sharing my enthusiasm for learning.

Research was another positive outcome of this newly acquired devotion to teaching. I realized that high-quality teaching could not occur behind closed doors in the classroom but could only happen if I expanded my horizons. The Internet became a daily resource where I harvested more for my basket. I searched for lesson plans and creative ideas from other teachers, but especially for opportunities to contribute my own creations. Soon several teacher- and student-based projects popped up, and shortly I found myself participating in different kinds of ventures that turned out to be successful. I used thematic units based on the state's curriculum to allow my creativity to run free.

While I was enjoying my projects, I came to realize that my students were experiencing the same kind of learning enterprise that triggered a passionate quest for knowledge in me. I introduced my students to group projects where they could inquisitively research and creatively present their findings. The discovery phase and the presenting phase (where teachers usually find their infatuation) became available to my students. They responded with true dedication, giving 100% of themselves. I can only tell you that witnessing fourth graders mimic my movements and changes in tone of voice while presenting their analysis proved to me that the passion for teaching and learning are connected and that they are both triggered by observation.

With the announcement of awards, the administration of my school opened the door of my classroom for other teachers to observe. However, in everything that they witnessed (good and bad, of course) there was always a common factor in their remarks: my passion for teaching. Observers came and left with renewed spirits. Many times I heard teachers say that they had "gained strength" by watching me. One even said that by observing me, she understood the importance of keeping the act of teaching alert, alive, and fresh all the time. Again, I was assured that the best avenue to impart my success to my colleagues was in the same way that I had learned: teaching was not to be prescribed but exemplified. As a result, two years after my first award, another teacher in my school was awarded as well.

This is my experience, which I by no means intend to put forth as the only avenue to success. In the same way, I urge you to take from my opened door what inspires you to fall in love with one of the most valuable professions of all. And why not share it with the teacher next door?

Helpful Tips

- Become passionate.
- Become infatuated with knowledge before expecting others to do so through you. Find that first step to feeding your imagination and curiosity for knowledge. Passion will come naturally, and in turn, it will be the creative force to keep you committed for the long term. Let lifelong learners inspire you.
- Learn how to be surprised and how to show surprise! Analyze how your body shows surprise and do not be afraid to use it.
- Have inspiring thoughts about teaching around your desk. Reflect on them often.
- Convince yourself that passionate teachers do not have a specific personality type: affection grows where it is fed.
- Model your passion.
- Take initiative: open your classroom door! Involve administration in the construction of a school culture that would advocate peer observation. Making your teaching public and not private will exhort you to be a better teacher; models cannot be mediocre.
- Separate the modelling of passion from peer evaluation; let spectators come to fill their cups and not to stir yours. Trust will take place.
- Bring gadgets to the classroom; they can turn on the power of a dull lesson.
- Use humor, use humor, and use humor! Brighten up a grammar lesson with silly examples.
- Feel confident in yourself; feel the joy of an artist learning to paint.

The Music Underlying the Words

Classroom Climate

Diane Marie Palmer-Furman
Denver, Colorado

The climate of a classroom is the atmosphere or feeling that pervades it daily. It is the music underlying the words—an energy that either contributes to or distracts from children's social development and opportunity to learn. A positive climate evolves out of

- An atmosphere of trust
- A sense of belonging and community
- Involvement in decision making
- Kindness and encouragement from peers
- Teacher and school staff's energy and morale
- The teacher and school staff's authenticity, fairness, and congruent communication to students and each other
- Clear expectations, goals, and learning outcomes

The Song of Room 201

Inside the red brick walls of our classroom, 26 students are eager to learn and share their knowledge with others. There is a positive feeling inside our room: an ambience of pride, determination, and empowerment is dominant. There is a definite sense of trust and a feeling of belonging among our community of learners. This is the strength that holds us together. The racial and cultural backgrounds of the students add different rhythms and beats to our song. As an educator, I work hard to ensure that my classroom harmonizes with its melodies. I also want parents to hear that same tune when they walk through our doors.

Composing the Music

The dynamics of my classroom atmosphere are trust, humor, respect, responsibility, and accountability. What I expect from my students is what I expect from myself. A teacher's personality and values are naturally put into play when conducting a classroom. My students are also bringing in their own individual personalities, experiences, and values. Bringing these together is a challenge I look forward to meeting. I must trust my students and the choices they make. Once this trust is established, my students own the learning that takes place. I try not to let my students feel as though they are submitting to external imposition, but rather that they are part of a working team that chooses to play the game of following rules and procedures. Rules, rituals, and routines have to be in place, and my students must know and adhere to these practices conducive to learning.

The Notes That Create the Music

Parents must also know the rules, rituals, and routines of my classroom. I could not be as effective if I didn't have the support of the parents. I transmit a strong belief about the critical role a family plays in the education of the child. Parents are an intricate part of the learning process that occurs in the lives of their children. Parents' ideas, thoughts, and knowledge of their child as a learner and member of our society contribute greatly to my own understanding of my students.

A commitment to continuous improvement in bridging the gap between home and school is an important component in my classroom. To bridge this gap I use a very positive and effective form of communication that creates a partnership between parent, student, and teacher. My Friday Folder forms an alliance that breaks the barriers to learning, establishes educational support for the student in the home, and strengthens accountability. My Friday Folder consists of a Friday Reflection sheet that has a number of important components.

Weekly Reflection

The weekly reflection is where the student evaluates his or her responsibilities for learning and social behaviors. This component allows parents and me to see how the children view themselves as learners. Students often write about their "new learning" and share their newly gained knowledge with their parents. This begins to create positive communication between parent and child. Parents have a better understanding of the curriculum and standards of our district.

Rubric Scoring Section

I designed a rubric scoring component because it was crucial for my students and their parents to see and understand my expectations for positive learning. The criteria also coincide with classroom expectations and rules.

- Listens when others are speaking
- Follows directions
- Uses time wisely
- Respects rights of others
- Completes assigned tasks
- Respects authority
- Reads independently

This criteria is scored on a scale from 0 to 4:

0 = unacceptable
1 = marginal
2 = satisfactory
3 = good
4 = excellent

Teacher Comments

Every Thursday evening I spend a large amount of time writing comments about the students' weekly progress and achievements or help for the student who may need support in a subject, strategy, or skill. I always start with positive comments so parents understand the strengths of their child. Many parents I work with do not have pleasant memories of their elementary school experience. Friday Folder Reflections help establish a constructive bridge between home and school. Students look forward to reading their scores and the comments I write. I see them become much more responsible in their learning behaviors because of Friday Reflections.

Student Evaluations

This year I have added a new component to our Friday Reflection. I wanted my students to evaluate themselves on three basic statements about homework, using their time for learning, and whether they are proud of their work. They answer "yes" or "no." If there are any discrepancies between our scores I conference with that student. This new component has increased communication between parent and child on the progress and effort the student is making in class.

Hearing the Music

By using Friday Reflection sheets as a self-evaluation tool for my students and for me, I have established a higher sense of responsibility and accountability in the classroom. Friday Reflections have made my students more aware of who they are as learners and the actions they need to take to do the best they can. It has brought independence to my students as learners and empowered them to have more control of their education, a concept many of them have not experienced in school. All children who enter my classroom must believe they are capable of learning. They must believe they have the power to change and remove any barriers that are in the way of success. The Friday Reflection has increased the achievement of my students because it has instilled motivation, determination, and confidence.

▨   Thank You, Mrs. Woodford

Diane Woodford
South Sioux City, Nebraska

Unique children arrive in my classroom every single year. Some are tall or short, gifted or challenged in some way, bubbling storytellers or quiet thinkers. The year I had Morgan Ray seemed no different.

My community had just restructured our school district. We had a new teaching staff, new students, and a new name on our vintage structure. As introductions were zipping around my classroom, Morgan connected only with her eyes and smile. The kids included her, but she remained quiet. Her silence took me by surprise as the other 28 students busied themselves rekindling relationships put on hold over the summer. Moving about the room, absorbing the energy of the first day of school, I knew something *was* different.

It was during the next activity that I called for a response from each child. When Morgan Ray's name was called, a choir of ten-year-olds responded, "She doesn't talk!" I cannot imagine the confused look I must have displayed. As the day progressed, Morgan Ray's silence was confirmed. She did not speak to anyone all day.

At home that night I started on the research; I read about selective mutism. The next day I checked out her cumulative records and wrote down all of her past teachers' names. Every contact I made was the same. Each educator admitted to having this bright child and no one ever heard her speak in school. She would record presentations at home. She would produce wonderful informational posters. She worked hard on her daily work and progressed through concepts with success. She was quiet through it all. She had an army of protectors who had known her since preschool. They spoke for her when there was an urgent need. She appeared independent; however, she relied totally on her classmates for contacts that required a voice.

My year with Morgan Ray was troubling. My classroom is a place where success is celebrated. Students are taught and expected to praise each other. Working collaboratively, students learn to master difficult concepts. When students display a special interest or talent in a content area, they are heralded as the experts to go to for assistance. All of this requires communication through the spoken word. Morgan Ray could speak and she did at home. At school she held the key to her silence with unwavering control. At some point in her life it had been a choice, but now it was not a changeable option for her. Several times it seemed as if the words were there ready to tumble out, but then she would show a sort of strength and remain quiet, choosing to write a note instead.

Can a silent student be part of a group? Morgan Ray found ways to be included in our room's climb toward excellence. The students had a sense of acceptance for Morgan's silence that protected her from ridicule. There was never a time when she became a target. She was always pleasant, accepting of others, and helpful. In some strange way she normalized her situation.

The whole year I worked to seek out different ideas that would maybe bring about a response. One word from Morgan Ray would have made me shout success from the mountain top. It never happened in the classroom. When she did not present orally, she had a consequence that she willingly accepted. My fight for Morgan's voice resulted in counseling for her during the school day by a specialist. That was our turning point. The moment she would get into the school van for her trip to the counselor, she would begin a conversation. I felt like an answer was close. The counselor admitted that progress was being made; however, it was likely that correction for this type of mutism might take months or years. My time with Morgan Ray was running short.

With the approach of the last day of school, my students made a goodbye video with the assistance of the principal. Morgan Ray was left alone with the video camera in the principal's office and told to leave a message for me. The office staff was not surprised to find that she was only in the office alone for seconds. Everyone assumed she just turned off the camera and left. Upon examining the tape, the unbelievable had happened. Morgan Ray left me a message with the most precious of words.

The principal allowed me to view the tape with Morgan Ray at my side. As I watched this young lady take a very brave step toward her future, I was overcome with emotion. Morgan Ray quietly said, "Thank you, Mrs. Woodford."

The first step is the hardest and now it was behind her. I asked her permission to share the tape with the whole class on the last afternoon of school. Every child had a message about fifth grade on that tape. As we progressed through the documentary, there was laughter and reminiscing going on. The students were wrapping up another year of school, so who could be expected to sit quietly? When Morgan's face came on the screen a few kids who were still attending to the video noticed her mouth move. One of my students truly screamed, "She talked! Can we replay that?" I looked at Morgan for permission. The whole room was shrouded in excited silence.

Then for the first time ever in school, her friends, protectors, and peers heard her lovely voice say, "Thank you, Mrs. Woodford." The room burst with cheers and applause. There was hugging, laughter, praise, compliments, and tears. These kids had shared a special moment that would remain on their minds for years to come. Morgan Ray could talk in school and we celebrated!

Morgan continues to work with a counselor. She went on to a new school that continues to set high expectations for her. Today she is doing fine.

This experience, more than any other in my teaching career, taught me to be persistent in looking for solutions. All children need to be held to high expectations, regardless of the challenges. All children need to be in a learning environment that promotes a positive mindset. All children need celebrations. The formula for success is different for each child. My choice is to let students know that I will be standing beside them as they climb toward excellence, and we will celebrate.

Helpful Tips

- Recognize achievement and celebrate it! There is nothing wrong with the phrase "Good Job!" Children love to hear it.
- The end is not mastery of a concept. Expect students to expand it, apply it, redirect it, share it, tweak it, or teach it to someone else.
- Learn about reading, writing, math, and social skills as if survival depends on mastery; it does.
- Be the bright spot in someone's day. Show appreciation. Be sure to compliment students, teachers, parents, the lunch ladies, the janitors, and anyone else in your school, and expect nothing in return. It feels good.
- Be kind and honest with everyone because it is the right thing to do.
- Smiling and whining are both contagious. One is a curse and the other is a cure. Keep smiling!
- It is right to have high expectations for all children.
- The habit of a positive attitude can make any situation a teachable moment.
- Believe in courage, curiosity, and confidence to do what others see as impossible.
- Encourage, create, and promote wonder. Wonder is thinking. Thinking leads to success.

▨ They Believe

Diane Woodford
South Sioux City, Nebraska

My students hear confirmations of their successes repeatedly throughout the school day. Is it corny to continuously praise students for achievement, effort, and cooperation? If the praise is focused and sincere, it can only heighten a student's efforts to continue on a path of excellence.

The world of school is a vibrant blend of strategies, personalities, and information. This micro-environment where education happens is always changing. Children are expected to bounce from one topic to another, change settings, change teachers, and achieve at or above grade level regardless of abilities or disabilities. How can we guarantee progress? A dynamic educator makes each child *believe*. This belief in self can empower most children to higher levels of success.

The way in which teachers refer to students can build a degree of belief. In content area classes, my students are not called boys and girls or fifth graders. To empower my students I refer to them as authors or editors when we are writing. In math class, they are mathematicians or accountants. In science class, they are scientists, geologists, doctors, or researchers. By taking on the professional persona, students think outside the 10-year-old body where they reside. From the time children are very small we role play. That drama has a place in every classroom where children believe in themselves.

I continue to brainstorm ways to make children believe. As an incentive to become better descriptive writers, the children use digital photography to enhance writings with photo illustrations. Each child is trusted to take care of the cameras. Each child is trusted to take appropriate pictures. This trust leads to a self-esteem boost. High quality pictures become part of the students' writing notebooks. Students from past years have continued to rewrite some of their original stories. This shows that they believe they are authors.

Surprisingly, an unexpected result of the digital photography has been a remarkable interest in PowerPoint presentations. Since we now have access to pictures of students working and performing, we can share our school day with others. Our school activities are no longer a secret; creative students capably design presentations for their parents and families. Connecting with families opens the door for strengthened parental support, a must for school success.

As a Teacher of the Year, I was given the opportunity to attend International Space Camp. The space camp experience included wearing a NASA flight suit. When the blue jumpsuit was zipped up, my astronaut personality clicked on. I believed I could accomplish astronaut-like feats on the simulators. My sense of self changed with the outfit.

In my classroom, students are now transformed into scientists in a similar way. With the help of my local PTA, my students are outfitted in science lab coats to accompany our investigations and experiments. The results are immediate. Students who rarely participated in the past are now actively engaging in the scientific process. By wearing the lab coats, they believed in their scientist status. They believed! That was the ultimate result.

Teaching students to believe becomes the focus of all successful teachers. Once students are on the path of achievement, a creative educator enhances the atmosphere by interjecting positive statements of sincere praise. Transforming classrooms into interactive environments of learning can happen with modern technology like digital photography or old-fashioned props like costuming. Celebrate mastery, praise, believe, and expect. Add to that kindness, honesty, smiles, and wonder. The foundation of success depends on this list. Quality educators share it with children to connect with the world outside the classroom. The result: children believe!

Perception, Focus, and Attitude

Teachers Leading the Way

Mary Catherine Bradshaw
Nashville, Tennessee

> *Human history becomes more and more a race between education and catastrophe.*
>
> —*Herbert George Wells*

Inadequate funding for all schools, overcrowded classrooms, mounds of administrative paperwork to satisfy accountability requirements, high attrition rates of young teachers from the classroom, marginal support for education at home, curriculum design, resegregation of schools across the country, standards-based education, discouraged teachers, special education needs, and school choice are all equally profound issues facing public education today. However, the most profound issue in public education is the perception that our schools are failing. Can we improve? Yes, always. Are we failing? No.

The extent to which public education has been politicized has had profoundly negative effects on public education. I have heard a United States Senator compare test scores of U.S. students to test scores of German and Japanese students and proclaim the U.S. students a failure. An uninformed listener might be alarmed that the U.S. students are falling short and that the country is in an education crisis. In reality, comparing those groups of students is similar to comparing apples and oranges. U.S. test scores from K–12 include all students; Japan's and Germany's scores include only the students who have been selected or allowed to stay in the system. When newspapers and politicians compare scores of magnet schools, charter schools, independent schools, and comprehensive high schools and claim that one school is superior to another or that one school is failing, the articles and speeches usually fail to point out the inherent differences in the student populations' ability levels and other admission requirements that might explain a dramatic difference in test scores.

Politicians need a rallying cry and negative news sells newspapers. Consequently, public education is an easy target because the patrons of K–12 education, the students and their families, move through the system and lose interest after they exit the system at the end of high school or earlier. Teachers and administrators are left to promote, sustain, and, at the present time, defend the system. The problem with this is that educators are and should be focused on teaching and learning, curriculum design, professional growth, and discovering what works best in our individual schools and classrooms. Educators are busy professionals who are not trained and typically not interested in political battles and power struggles. Unfortunately, the effect of this "manufactured crisis," as David Berliner and Bruce Biddle call it, is the perception that public schools are failing. The irony is that the more often schools are promoted as inadequate and the more often educators are left to defend our efforts, the more likely schools are to suffer. Middle class families abandon comprehensive high schools for charter schools, magnets, and independent schools because they perceive them to be better. What is left? After a steady attrition of students, the tipping point occurs and comprehensive high schools are a struggling shell of their former selves. Test scores are used to show more failures and schools are labeled as failing. This cycle is self-perpetuating. Politicians and the media have capitalized on the data and now we really have a problem, but it is a problem of perception, not failure.

What might be done to change public perception? Educators are going to have to be more vocal about our own successes, not just about inadequate pay and how overworked we are. We need to rise up and claim the success that is ours. By claiming and defining our successes we will help to change perceptions and reestablish the legitimacy of all types of public schools, not just magnets and charter schools. Educators must also demand a broader system of accountability than just test scores. This nation did not become and has not remained the major, and some believe the only, world power if its public education system is a failure. Are we finished and do we have the "final answer"? No, of course not, public education is not a game of *Who Wants to Be a Millionaire?* or "Who wants to be elected and have the power"? It is a process of research, reflection, and responsiveness that demands time, energy, and respect if it is to continue to flourish. Educators must take the lead in demanding what we need and tempering the impact of the manufactured crisis of the media and the politicians; it is something we should not have to do, but we must or catastrophe will win the race, not education.

We are at a critical point in the history of public education in America. Politicians and media continue to frame education discussions around the idea of failing public schools. Cries and policies to "leave no child behind" resonate in political speeches, newspapers, and policy making. I asked my grandmother, who is 97 and taught school for several years, what she thought the major problem in education is today. She said, "The people who are making the rules aren't the people who know about classrooms. They are too far removed to know what works." I am inclined to agree. They don't know what works, and they fail to see the big picture by making evaluations based primarily on test scores.

In 1971, the percentage of 25- to 29-year-old high school graduates who had attended some college or who had received a Bachelor's degree or higher was 44%, compared to 62% in 1995, which is the most recent data that I have found. College completion, which is defined as receiving some type of Bachelor's degree, increased more modestly from 22% in 1971 to 28% in 1995. The graphs for the ethnic breakdown of these increases illustrate gains for Hispanics, whites, and blacks. Composite ACT scores in 1970 were 18.6 compared to 21.0 in 2001. Between 1979 and 2000, U.S. crime rates dropped. The recent *Advanced Placement Report to the Nation 2005* indicates that a higher percentage of students take AP courses. In 2000, 15.9% of the nation's students took AP tests compared to 20.9% in 2004. In 2000, 10.2% of the AP exam takers demonstrated college-level mastery compared to 13.2% in 2004. This data suggest sustained improvement to me, not failure. Why isn't that in the news?

I would challenge all educators to demand a new message from the policy makers and the media. Do we still have work to do? Yes. Can we continue to find ways to enhance the opportunities for learning and success for our students? You bet, but first we must insist on reframing the rhetoric and look at the amazing successes of public education in more realistic terms rather than the minutiae of test scores.

Educators must speak and write as often as we can to parents, students, politicians, media people, community leaders, alumni, citizens, and each other about the gains, not the losses; the successes, not the failures; and the opportunities, not the vacuums. We must do this collectively and immediately if we are to preserve one of the cornerstones of participatory American democracy: public education.

Accepting the Challenge

Nancy K. Ackerman
Santa Teresa, New Mexico

When I was a little girl there was no doubt in my mind that I would grow up to be an educator. My mother, Irene McAuliffe, taught for 39 years in the El Paso public school system, and she was most definitely my inspiration for becoming a teacher. When I was growing up, I was fortunate to have the opportunity to visit my mother's classes. I watched my mother as she taught predominantly Spanish-speaking children how to read and write in English. I watched as she bandaged skinned knees and patched bruised egos. I went with her to visit students who were ill and saw how readily the families accepted her into their homes. I noted the loving rapport between my mother, her students, and their parents, and I knew that when I grew up I wanted to be just like her. I feel such tremendous pride in this beautiful lady who loved her profession so much. She led the way for me and I will be eternally grateful to her.

I, along with my colleagues, have the most challenging and most demanding profession on the planet. No matter what obstacles confront us, we know in our hearts that we must help each and every one of our students to achieve his or her potential.

I believe that each child comes to school with his or her own unique set of special needs. Academic needs range from exceptionally slow learners to gifted and talented students. This range places special demands upon us that we must be able to satisfy. Children's personal needs are equally demanding. In education today, we must be ready to deal with abusive home situations, children or parents with drug problems, gang violence, and single-parent homes. I believe, and very strongly I might add, that these issues are challenges to be met and overcome, not excuses for being unable to teach our students.

With all of the various needs of our students in mind, I try first to make sure that the children know they are in a safe, secure environment. I purposely spend a lot of time on building community so that my students feel free to ask any question and be risk takers. I want every child to have a positive attitude toward learning and I want our classroom to be an inviting and exciting place to be. I provide a differentiated curriculum that includes depth and complexity so that my students are always striving for knowledge. We are a community of learners who care about each other and are eager to face new challenges together.

Parents are an extremely important part of our team. I encourage parents to come to our class as often as possible. Parents have a wealth of knowledge and experience to share, and I want them to feel welcome in our classroom. I have devised a method for communicating with parents that allows us to speak every day. I send a homework folder with small notes from me daily and a quarterly letter to explain our intended curriculum for the grading period. They are encouraged to get in touch with me whenever they have questions or if they feel that they have expertise in any of the areas we intend to cover during the year. We have had parents in the classroom showing us how to make paper, drawing the human body, telling the history of their mother country and teaching us some of their language, and doing origami. What an asset to our classroom our parents have been. Upon completion of a project, parents are always invited to help us celebrate. When the students arrive at my classroom door, I feel as if they are part of my family. My family has grown quite large over the last 28 years.

Teaching is my passion. In order to do the best possible job, I, too, must continually be learning. I keep up with the latest innovations in our field by attending training sessions, seminars, conferences, and classes. I have an extensive library of professional materials, which I enjoy every bit as much as a good novel. In order to be an effective educator, I feel that I must also keep up with the latest methodologies. Not only is learning important, but also sharing that knowledge with our colleagues is equally important. I am totally committed to the concept of "team." Our campuses should make sure that all administrators, staff, teachers, parents, and children work together toward our common goal of successfully educating our children.

When I went to work for the Gadsden Independent School District, little did I realize that I would be facing the biggest challenge of my career. My mother was born in the Mesilla Valley where I am now teaching. My grandfather, in 1917, chose to move his family to the big city of El Paso to ensure a good education for his children. I never dreamed how this family history would shape my future.

For a very long time, New Mexico has had a less than perfect record of educating its populace. Some of New Mexico's educational challenges are unique to our being a border community. In the southeastern area of our state, the Mesilla Valley where my mother's family grew up, we have many students who are new arrivals to the United States. Our population is very transient as our families migrate back and forth across the border. Maintaining proficiency in reading is difficult under these circumstances. Home-school communication is complicated as well, and that bond is essential to foster reading programs that work. When I came to the Gadsden Independent School District, I found that the reading program varied throughout the district and throughout my own campus. Our district test scores were down, and we needed to look for a reading initiative that would meet children's and teachers' needs. I was appalled to find that my students were a part of that scenario, and I had to rely on prior experience to help my students succeed. The approach I used is called the Balanced Literacy Approach.

About the same time, Gadsden District chose to meet its literacy challenges by implementing a *districtwide* reading approach. The Balanced Literacy Approach was the instrument they chose. The curriculum is adjusted to meet each child's needs. Assessment takes place daily and that assessment drives instruction. Because children are reading at their own level of ability, they are able to make the connections so vital for comprehension and, therefore, they progress successfully and quickly.

After two years of piloting the Balanced Literacy Approach at Desert View Elementary, our District Management Team asked all of the principals in the district to decide whether they would like to implement this approach at their campuses. The principals overwhelmingly agreed to begin the Balanced Literacy Approach in their schools at the beginning of the 2003–2004 school year, and we are now all on the same sheet of music. Part of the program was to have Reading Process Trainers at each of the 14 campuses in the District. I decided that I had a personal interest because of my heritage and I had the expertise to be of help; therefore, I applied for the position of Reading Process Trainer.

It was an honor to be selected as a member of the Balanced Literacy Team. Thirteen trainers and I have been assigned to specific campuses where we will be training our teachers in Balanced Literacy methodologies. All 14 of us have received extensive training and will continue to attend training sessions to be as effective as possible for our teachers. I find myself modeling different strategies at different grade levels to facilitate learning a new program not only for our teachers, but for our students as well.

Mrs. Yturralde, the principal of Desert View Elementary, and Ms. Lorna Clarke, a kindergarten teacher from Desert View, were invited to the White House for the 2005 State of the Union Address to represent the success of our Balanced Literacy Program, which addresses the No Child Left Behind legislation. Our children are learning, our teachers are learning, and I am so very proud to be a member of such a forward-thinking district.

My last words would be to my grandfather. "We are fixing it, Grandpa. None of our children will ever again have to move from their New Mexico home to get a better education."

CHAPTER 6

Empowering Students as Leaders

 **Each One, Teach One**

Ernest Schiller
Donnellson, Iowa

Teachers, wow, what a resource we are forgetting to use! I know that many of you are much like me, way too busy to get help—even if that help sits right in one of our classrooms. Well, at my school, Central Lee High School, when I find a student who knows more than I do, I use that student. As a matter of fact, when I find a student who knows more than I do, I accept that fact as a real advantage for my class. As teachers, we sometimes don't use our surrounding resources wisely. I use those students who have developed an expertise in their field of interest as an immediate resource. Such students can both elicit their peers' interest in the topic and bring an energy level to the classroom that normally might not exist. As a matter of fact, when I determine that one of my students has developed a knowledge and understanding of the biological principles that is deeper than my own interest and understanding, I become a better educator.

It is okay for the students to know more than the instructor. We instructors seem to want to hold sole control over the subject or subjects that we teach. We think that our curriculum is best understood by us, but I am living proof that it is okay for students to know and understand more than I do about a scientific principle through their own personal interest and their own personal scientific research. In this case, we can elicit further understanding by using peer assistance with obstacles to instruction and learning.

My philosophy of teaching is to raise the level of expectation of students in my science classes, to encourage them to become scientifically literate, and to enable them to make decisions based on their science background. This philosophy is reiterated by my dedication to the idea of *each one, teach one;* I designate student peer leaders in the classroom. Student peer leaders are students who have developed expertise in a particular area of science. Peer leaders are used in my classroom in classroom discussions, as laboratory assistants, and as research specialists (especially if the student has developed an extensive scientific research project, as several students at Central Lee have).

Using students as resident experts has proven immensely successful. Through peer interactions, students see science in a different light and think about career choices and career options that I would never have been able to create. The peer interactions also help to clear up misconceptions about the explanations that I give.

Several of my students have become superior science researchers in their own right. They have assimilated knowledge from classroom discussions, laboratories, and cooperative learning activities and have used that knowledge in their own scientific practice, much like professional researchers in universities and research corporations. Peer student researchers share their knowledge of their science topic, their research protocol, and their apparent love for the science principles that they are studying. My students enjoy learning from their peers. Peer scientists are also great and immediate role models for younger science students.

My science students enjoy listening to seminars and discussions with their classmates. They truly enjoy employing the principal of *each one, teach one.*

To Russia With Love

Evan D. Mortenson
Klamath Falls, Oregon

It was just last minute shopping at a mall before the new school year began, but who would have imagined that it would turn into a project that would involve so many people from our own community, our school, and the entire state of Oregon. I could only dream that so many would become so deeply united in a common cause.

While browsing in a department store one afternoon, I wondered why a gentleman at the clothing rack, jacket in hand, kept cycing me then looking questioningly at the item that he held. Finally, he approached and explained that he was purchasing the coat for a man who lived in Russia whom he had not yet been able to meet. He informed me that after looking at the man's photograph, he believed that we were about the same size. Of course, this piqued my curiosity, and I just had to know how he had made an acquaintance in such a far-off land.

Mr. Saunders and his wife had viewed a national broadcast in which children in Russia were asked what they would like Santa Claus to bring them if they had a Christmas wish. One little girl, Valya Baranova, said that she would like to have a pair of winter boots for her older sister, Galya, who had outgrown her own boots and was forced to wear her father's old ones to school. The Saunders were touched by the selflessness of the 11-year-old, and were eventually able to make contact with her. Their question to her was what would she like to have for herself. Her response: a felt pen for school or perhaps a pencil box. Valya's father, a fireman, earns the equivalent of U.S. $10 a month, and her mother, a nurse, earns about $12 a month, so common items are not easy to come by. Many supplies are simply nonexistent in a small rural community such as theirs. It was at about this point in the discussion that I realized that this was potentially a great school-community project. I asked whether my students could become involved by starting a pen pal program. The Saunders were thrilled at the idea, but already I had thoughts that we might do more than just write letters.

By the end of October, I was able to address the parents of our students at a school booster meeting. I recounted the events that had lead me to this point and explained that my own students wanted to send Christmas cards to the Russian children at Valya's school. They felt that this would allow them to better understand and appreciate the value of their own school, education, and circumstances. It would also provide an opportunity for service unlike any we had previously encountered. I asked whether the parents would help with a fundraiser to buy postage for the cards. I also suggested that if we had enough money, it would be nice to send some felt pens. The chairman asked whether they would support the initiative. There was a moment of silence, then one of the mothers stood and said it was not good enough. She suggested that we ask local businesses to become involved with the school as well. Suddenly, a dozen parents were anxiously engaged in the conversation. Many had local contacts and were planning to make phone calls and personal visits as soon as the meeting adjourned.

Committees were formed to investigate donations, and others were assigned to check with delivery companies just to see how difficult sending items might be. Others volunteered to check with the Russian Embassy in San Francisco to see what supplies would be allowed into the country and what duty or taxes might be imposed. One parent suggested that the entire student body make Christmas cards and personalize them with a short letter and a photograph. Everyone had a task to do, and all were excited beyond anything I had ever seen.

The very next afternoon another meeting was held. Already the news was encouraging. The committee chairman had gone to speak with the manager of the local Wal-Mart the night of the booster meeting. As they talked about the project, the manager looked enthusiastic, yet sad. He informed our chairman that their store had just selected all their charity programs and had used up their donation allotment for the Christmas season. He said that he would see what they could do. Some of their office staff overheard the plan for our project, and the very next morning Wal-Mart called a staff meeting at which the details were discussed. Even though the store charity funds were already spoken for, every single employee volunteered to purchase a pencil box and fill it with school supplies. To our surprise, these great people purchased nearly 150 pencil boxes.

Cases of pencils, pens, rulers, and myriad assorted school items began to appear at the school. A local newspaper reporter heard of the event and came to the school to ask the students and staff for more details. When an article in the local paper was printed, supplies and donations overwhelmed us. K-Mart and Gottschalks employees donated other items such as gloves, socks, and candy to send to their newfound friends. Money was donated to fund the postage. Letters of appreciation from well-wishers flooded the school. A reporter from the wire service called the school for permission to run the story statewide. Soon a printed article appeared in the Eugene and Portland newspapers, closely followed by generous donations to students and a little school that nobody had ever heard of before. Dozens of letters arrived from people in the big cities. Some of them were Russian emigrants who praised our children and the community for their efforts and kindness. In short order the project had nearly $1,300 in funding.

A booster meeting in December focused on the many obstacles that faced the delivery of the items. A parent reported that the Russian Embassy required a steep tariff on the supplies being sent. This same parent contacted a congressman in California about the project. The congressman met with the Russian ambassador and the tariff was dropped. Another parent reported that the delivery company, DHL, agreed to send the items for a limited charge, but we would need to take the boxes to Sacramento, 350 miles away. We had many who volunteered to make the trip. For every hurdle someone would step up and solve the problem. We also had the challenge of delivery to the Russian school in Chereneva Nalya, a small farming community about 300 miles north of the Caspian Sea. The six boxes of supplies would be sent on a fantastic nine-day journey in December from Klamath Falls, Oregon to Sacramento to Washington, D.C.; London; Frankfurt; Moscow; and eventually the small town of Malika some 150 miles from the Valya's home and school. The last leg of the trip would be to have the delivery picked up by Mr. Baranova in his small car.

The first week of December we held an all-school assembly to make all of the Christmas cards by hand. Each student made his or her own card and included a letter and a photo. We also included a pencil box for each teacher full of things that they might find useful in their classrooms. The individual pencil boxes were filled by students along an assembly line, then personalized with their cards and letters. We had spent weeks researching everything that we could about the people of Russia, their government, lifestyle, and economics. We learned much about the community that would be the recipient of our care package. A parent offered to help us make a poster with a photo of our school, students, and staff. It included postcards of our rural community showing the many similarities between our homes. We included a map to show where we are located in the United States.

Then the big day came; we sent our presents off. Each day the students nearly fought over tracking the package by computer, and they became impatient when the shipment was delayed in Germany for two days, then in Moscow for three days. But a loud cheer filled the school the morning when it showed up on the screen that the boxes were "Received by customer."

A few weeks later we received photos from the disposable cameras that we included in the packages along with return postage. The first picture was of the Baranova's little car, with four of the boxes tied to the top of the vehicle. They were covered in snow, yet they made the trip safely. Then my students got their first view of the faces of the students they had been trying to learn more about. Some parents wept as they studied the pictures of each Russian classroom and its students holding up their new gifts.

There are many avenues to involve a community in the school system, yet this project seemed to be magic. It succeeded because of the well-planned efforts of a parent-school partnership as well as the devotion of the community. I have seldom seen such purpose in the eyes of my students. These young people were learning firsthand about others outside their own little world. They developed a dimension of caring that they had never experienced before; they were the hands of friendship to a community on the other side of the world.

Helpful Tips

- I have found that encouraging parent-teacher-community involvement is much easier through a service project.
- I am not fond of fundraisers as a way to involve parents and community. They are more of a means to an end and must support a project of greater value.
- Parent groups such as Boosters and PTA seem to be more effective than school Site Councils in getting things done. Site Councils have a different focus than the other groups but often have most of the same people working on them.
- Have a clear plan. Be sure that the end is in sight. It is a sad experience to begin a project that only gets half way.
- Allow parents to be the leaders in such a project.
- Always remember the saying, "That which is rewarded will get done." Make sure that volunteers at all stages are thanked and complimented for their efforts and successes. Cards are a great way to accomplish this.

📚 Using Children's Books in the High School Setting

Rita Cannon Hovermale
Bridgeville, Delaware

If I could wave my magic wand and make one thing happen for every child across this country, it would be to have a caring adult to read to him or her daily. Unfortunately, I doubt this will ever happen.

Students enter my high school classroom without the reading skills necessary to succeed in school, let alone prosper in the ever-changing workforce. After they've suffered years of frustrating reading experiences, getting students to read, let alone enjoy reading, is considered an impossible task by many high school teachers. In my early childhood education classes I have had great success in getting high school students to read children's books. For many, it is an opportunity to read at their reading level without fear of ridicule. Dr. Seuss provides the same enjoyment for a 16-year-old as he does for a four-year-old; in many cases the older children appreciate him more. High school students are able to grasp the underlying message that is only seen as silly to a preschooler.

Children's stories are also great ice breakers. They are silly enough that students don't laugh at each other but at each other's stories. When students lose the fear of failure and its accompanying ridicule, they can easily settle down to the task at hand.

Read Across America, a celebration of reading and of Dr. Seuss's birthday, is a great time to get students reading. High schools can celebrate the day by getting faculty members to read their favorite children's story at the beginning of class. There are so many great children's books available that any subject area can be covered.

Reading children's stories allows students to practice rate and fluency. Perfecting a children's story may seem like a waste of time to many high school teachers. However, without these skills, reading is difficult. Try getting students to practice and then read a children's story into a tape recorder. Have them listen and critique themselves and each other. These book/tape collections can then be given to elementary schools for children to use independently.

Since reading and writing are natural extensions of each other, have students write and illustrate their own children's story. Using rhythm and rhyme was Dr. Seuss's greatest asset, and it can work for high school students as well. These student-authored books can be related to a content area or a specific topic of study. In a similar vein, *School House Rock* is a perfect example of how using rhythm and rhyme can help with retention of somewhat dull or uninteresting material. Several generations of students still remember "Conjunction Junction" and the other episodes of this award-winning series.

Taking an original story or retelling an old favorite using sock puppets also forces students to delve deeper into the meaning of a story. Using old socks whose mates have been eaten by the washer, along with a little felt and glue, is an inexpensive way to allow students to bring the characters in stories to life. Many students are performers at heart; this gives them the chance to use that energy in a constructive fashion.

We have become so overwhelmed with accountability and testing that we have often lost sight of the potential for "fun" in education. We have taken the joy out of learning and replaced it with the job of learning. Reading and writing have become viewed as punishment administered by teachers. Using children's stories helps to rekindle the love of a good book. It helps to remind students of earlier times when each day was a new adventure and there were new things to learn. And for some students it can be their first positive interaction with the printed word.

Index

**CORWIN
PRESS**

The Corwin Press logo—a raven striding across an open book—represents the union of courage and learning. Corwin Press is committed to improving education for all learners by publishing books and other professional development resources for those serving the field of PreK–12 education. By providing practical, hands-on materials, Corwin Press continues to carry out the promise of its motto: **"Helping Educators Do Their Work Better."**